The King and The Moat Contractor
Strategy, Business Planning and Marketing
"For All Businesses and Industries"

By

Ronald A. McKenzie, Architect
COMPASS Consultants Corporation

The King and The Moat Contractor Strategy, Business Planning and Marketing "For All Businesses and Industries"

The King and the Moat Contractor is an on-going story that uses the construction industry as a platform to discuss strategy, business planning, and marketing, including business development. But the lessons apply to all businesses and industries, and to all who aspire to be the very best moat contractor or even King, if you have what it takes. The book is not a textbook, but is meant to get you to think about strategy and planning and marketing, as so often, textbooks miss the thinking part.

By

Ronald A. McKenzie, Architect
COMPASS Consultants Corporation

Published by D.E.M. Publishing,
A Division of COMPASS Consultants Corporation

For information, please contact:
COMPASS Consultants Corporation
ramckenzie.compass@gmail.com

The King and The Moat Contractor
Strategy, Business Planning and Marketing
"For All Businesses and Industries"

Published by D.E.M. Publishing,
A Division of COMPASS Consultants Corporation
"A Competitive Advantage Company"

For information, please contact:
COMPASS Consultants Corporation
Ronald A. McKenzie
ramckenzie.compass@gmail.com

ISBN 978-0-578-15185-4
Printed in the United States of America
10 9 8 7 6 5 4 3 2 1
First Edition

UNDERSTANDING

This publication is intended to provide useful information regarding the subject of business management and planning in a lighthearted manner. This is a fiction book that uses fictitious characters to make a point, hence, names, characters, places and incidents are a product of the author's imagination and are used fictitiously. Occasionally, quotations are used and the author has given credit; any omission is accidental and not intentional. Neither the author or the publisher assume any responsibility for any errors or omissions, nor do they represent or warrant the information, ideas, plans, actions, and suggestions. The book is marketed/sold with the understanding that the book is a platform for learning, and different situations require different individualized solutions. The author and the publisher specifically disclaim any liability resulting from the use or application of information contained in this book. There is an occasional guest appearance by the author, and other authors and business/marketing executives, as well as references to real events, businesses, organizations, and locales, are all intended to give this business material a sense of reality and authenticity.

DEDICATION

"Dedicated to all my clients who have helped me
become a better consultant."

To my wife, **Pamela S. McKenzie**, who always supports my writing.

To **Donald E. McKenzie**, (1946-2008), my identical twin brother
and writing partner, forever.

ACKNOWLEDGEMENTS

MANY PEOPLE are owed a great deal of thanks for their help and assistance, as I developed these <u>The King and the Moat Contractor Books</u> — my business associates, friends and clients have all supported my business efforts.

First, I must thank George Demarakis who created the caricatures of The King, Slide Rule and the Moat Contractor. George's artistic ability is beyond compare, and he is the first person I go to when I need illustrations of any kind to help me convey my ideas and concepts.

I would also like to thank Pamela of My Advertising Partner, Inc., who contributed her exceptional talents bringing George's artistic characters, the written content and graphic layout of this book to life.

<u>The King and the Moat Contractor</u> columns have appeared in several construction industry publications, but eventually found a home in **Metal Architecture**, who faithfully published my monthly thoughts for almost seven years. I thank everyone I have worked with at the magazine for their efforts. I also thank the many loyal readers and fans who sent me notes about the ideas I expressed.

I also want to thank all of the Kings and Queens I have met in the course of business, as well as all of the Moat Contractors and Architects. They have all contributed in some way to my visions of a better business world.

FOREWORD

The King and the Moat Contractor started off as a column in a magazine. An editor contacted me and asked me to contribute a column, so I wrote a conventional column that everyone is so familiar with, which many times are not read. I then asked the editor to wait, as I'm going to send a different version of the same column in about three days. It was then that I rewrote the article creating the very first **King and the Moat Contractor**. I emailed the article to them, and they liked it and decided to publish in their next magazine edition.

My tactic was simple; the way most people read magazines is they scan the article titles, then the bolded subsections and callouts, and sometimes read, if a phrase or idea catches their eye, but more often than not, continue to scan the magazine. It was my intent to create interest – I needed a hook. Who could not be drawn into a story about the King, who represented the **OWNER** of the Castle, the moat **CONTRACTOR** named Igor and the **ARCHITECT** named Slide Rule.

With those three characters I now had the vehicle for communicating my business planning ideas as they included the owner, the contractor and the architect, the three main players in most construction projects. As it was a parody, I talked about computers and tradeshows, which were referred to as "future things."

After publication the magazine received several emails commenting on the story as the ideas were helpful and entertaining, so the magazine asked me to write a second column ... and then a third. **The King and the Moat Contractor** was published in a couple magazines before finding a home with **Metal Architecture**. It appeared in the back as a monthly column and then eventually was moved to the front, and then to the lead column where it remained for almost six years! As a note to readers, if you want time to go by fast, sign up to write a monthly column!

Through the lectures of the King to Slide Rule the architect, and Igor the contractor, I have been able to explore strategic, business and marketing planning as well as business development, by telling stories and quoting many notable authors. **The King's lessons applies to all business and industries because they must also think, plan, and market.** I even wrote a sonnet, which is probably the first sonnet ever printed in a construction magazine.

Many of the stories are based upon my own experiences. For example, I went to a chiropractor, so the King went to a chiropractor, I went on a diet, and the King, Slide and Igor all went on a diet. Each story, whether it was about a diet, or going to a chiropractor lead to an important business planning concept. The messages in my columns have been consistent over the last six plus years. The King always lectured Slide Rule and Igor on the virtues of business planning, and by setting goals and objectives and by measuring results, you can control your firm's destiny.

UNDERSTAND: Planning gives you the tools to react to the signs of the economy and to competitive threats, and by constantly positioning your firm and providing real VALUE that goes well beyond the expressed needs and wants of the prospect, you can become victorious over your competition. Remember, if you don't plan and set benchmarks, you have nothing to measure against what actually happened.

The following quote has been attributed to many authors:

"The business of business, is business."

It's not a whimsical statement, but a serious suggestion that, in fact, many principals do not work ON their business, they work IN their business. By embracing the business planning philosophy, and working ON your business, you will be in a much better position than your competition. This means that at the end of the year, or your financial year, time must be reserved to address planning issues for next year. An orchestrated set of goals and objectives are reviewed in light of the economy, past years performance and what is expected the following year. But more important, issues facing the company are identified, prioritized, and discussed. **It is the conversations in the business planning process that are so valuable.**

The King is a master planner, as the act of planning pulls together a company so that they have a common direction and focus, while working to develop strengths, minimize weaknesses, develop opportunities and overcome threats. These concepts are interwoven into all the King articles, as the King leads his two subjects, Slide Rule the Architect, and Igor the Moat Contractor.

It must be understood that strategy is strategy, planning is planning, and marketing is marketing. **The lessons of the King are in the context of the**

construction world, but they apply equally to all business and industries that are looking to grow.

People are the most important asset, and too often, it is the people that managers sometimes forget about, as they take the heed of the finance department, and fire people so that bonuses can be made and a good year can be celebrated, not realizing that it's the people that got them there. They also don't realize that their negative actions start a slow spiraling downward trend as marketing and business development expenses are cut.

Now the popular trend is to cut people's hours back (saving money on insurance in some cases) and put business developers on commission only plans, which ironically contribute to the death spiral. Planning takes the position that marketing and business development are PART of the business, and those that see and understand this force are the ones that win the project, or come out with a new product or new service.

This is the reason why some companies experienced an increase in business in the last seven years during the economic downturn, and others barely survived or failed. You read that last line correctly. I have clients who have prospered very well during the last seven years. They planned, implemented, and never looked back.

"One of the dirty little secrets of marketing is you must want it to happen. You must have the eye of the tiger. The second little dirty secret of marketing is some <u>think</u> they have it, but they don't."

Using this book as a guide, the principal or sales manager, or marketing or business development director can have a conversation of the concepts in the book and apply them to your business. Having them read one article for the next meeting is not an overwhelming task. (Although shockingly, I had a principal of an architectural firm tell me that he doesn't read anything as it was a waste of time). Improvement is a series of small changes made over time, and if your firm doesn't do it, then do it for yourself.

Or better yet, call me. Let's talk. Let me help you develop a strategic, business and marketing plan, or re-work the ones you have. You see, I know a secret that you don't know. If you want the answer, call me or send me an email: ramckenzie.compass@gmail.com

I wish all my readers continued business success. I hope that I've helped you reach your business goals and to think of planning as an important part of your business.

One last point, in business, as in life, you must always pause for a moment and step back and reflect on the big picture which will provide you with the proper perspective for you to grow and prosper, both as a person and as a business.

Ronald A. McKenzie, NCARB
Architect. Author. Advisor.

TABLE OF CONTENTS

"IGOR AND SLIDE. PLEASE JOIN ME," said the King.
"Let me tell you a story I heard a long time ago."

THE CHARACTERS

THE KING, is the all knowing King and Owner of the Castle. His word is final, and his ideas are real world practical tactics.

IGOR is the Moat Contractor and Owner of Moat Designs, Ltd.

SLIDE RULE, referred to as **SLIDE,** is the No.1 architect for the Castle, and owner of Building Blocks, Inc.

THE BEGINNING

"IGOR AND SLIDE. PLEASE JOIN ME," said the King. "Let me tell you a story I heard a long time ago."

Igor and Slide took a seat with the King in a Pub at the end of a long hard day of work. Ale was served, first to the King, and then to Slide and Igor. "I love a good story," said Slide.

"Before I begin, There's a question I've always wanted to ask you. Igor, your company's name is Moat Designs, Ltd., but you're a contractor. You sound like a design firm. And Slide, your company's name is Building Blocks, Inc. You sound like a builder. Why is that?"

"That's a very astute observation," said Slide. "This column is a parody, and the brilliant author, architect, and advisor, Ron McKenzie, (shameless self–promotion), is making the statement that contractors try and move into the design arena so they can attract more business, while architects fancy themselves as builders, and hence, we have design/build. He's playing with words to get people to think about their business name."

"Really, said the King. "That's fascinating. Should be in a book."

PART I
STRATEGY

The Strategic Plan provides direction for a company and its employees for five-to-seven years based upon developing a company strategy of where your company wants to be in terms of positioning in your marketplace, meaning, there is a need to re-align the firm with a new vision. It includes a strategic analysis of your market, your strengths, your key factors for success, and how you deliver your services. A strategic plan may or may not be driven by company growth in terms of dollars, and a strategic plan may completely re-position your firm so you can compete effectively.

THE BUSINESS PATH TO GROWTH AND PROFIT

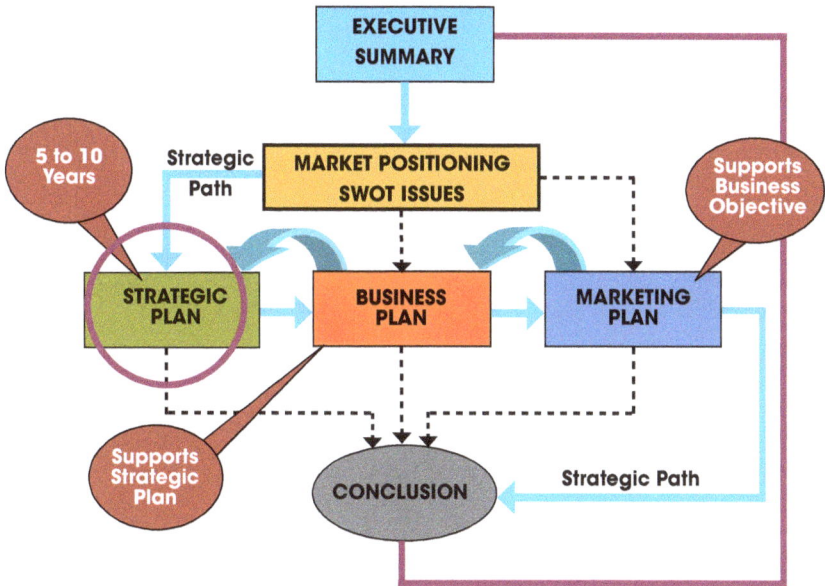

Fig. 1 The Business Planning Process – Strategy

17

STORY #1
Rich Cow, Poor Cow

IT'S A BEAUTIFUL DAY AT THE CASTLE. The King and his usual entourage of Knights and servants had left the Castle and were visiting the King's stockade. Joining him were Slide Rule of Building Blocks, Inc, the King's No. 1 architect, and Igor, the contractor for the Castle and owner of Moat Designs, Ltd.

Behind a fence were two cows. One cow was absolutely beautiful – its coat was almost polished and it was obviously well fed for it was well filled out. The other cow was sickly looking and had seen harder times for its ribs stuck out. The cow's eyes were hollow and looked scared, whereas the other cow looked comfortable and well.

"So," the King said. "What do you see here?"

"One cow is sick and the other one well," answered Slide. "I agree" said Igor.

The King nodded his head in agreement. "Actually, they are sisters."

"What happened?" asked Igor.

"This is the case of the Rich Cow and the Poor Cow."

"Okay. But what happened to create this?"

"When they were born I gave one of the cows to a sharecropper to raise and to use the milk for their family. Last week I went down to visit the family and this is what I found."

"That's terrible," commented Slide. Igor nodded his head in agreement.

"My cow, or course was well fed and I actually had her groomed everyday. The sick cow is a testimony to the sharecroppers selfishness."

Slide had been thinking and finally spoke up. "Perhaps this shows what happens when you don't have money."

The King thought about this and shook his head. "No, I think you're wrong. This has nothing to do with money and has everything to do with respect."

"In what way your Majesty?" Slide asked.

"Well, while it's true this appears to be a case of Rich Cow, Poor Cow, it really is about responsibility and respect. Slide, have you ever had a tough time in your business, and finally after a lot of work, you landed a new client."

"Yes, of course. We have all experienced that," answered Slide.

"What kind of service did you provide for them?" asked the King.

"I gave them the best service I could possibly provide. I couldn't afford it, but it was not in me to provide less than my very best."

"How about you Igor? There are a lot of ways to cut corners in construction. When you were starting out, and I know you were poor, did you cheat your customer?"

"Absolutely not. I will always do my best. I always do more then I have ever been asked."

"That's the reason I hired both of you. Responsibility and respect. You see, to reap what you sow is to experience the results of your own actions. I gave a cow to a sharecropper so he would have milk for his family, and this is what I get in return."

"It's almost as if the sharecropper did it to you personally," said Igor.

"Yes, you're right. Very good observation Igor. If I may go on. This is particularly true in business, and one of the more important business lessons to learn. It doesn't take long for the marketplace to find out what you're truly made of. If you pass the marketplace's test then your business will improve and you will reap what you sow. If you cut corners, it will show, as this cow demonstrates, and the marketplace will turn against you and you will be no more."

"What are you going to do, your Majesty?"

"Well, I own the land the sharecropper farms. I have told him to pack up and move on. He's going to reap what he sowed. I'm also going to take care of this cow and see that it becomes well and happy. I have a goal. Care to guess?"

"I don't know," said Slide.

"How about you, Igor?"

"I also take a pass on this one, your Majesty."

"The answer is simple. "Rich Cow, Poor Cow, is going to become "Rich Cow, Rich Cow.""

Every suspect, prospect, client, ally, employee, friends and family are to be treated with respect.

STORY #2
The Enemy

THE KING PACED BACK AND FORTH in the courtyard in front of the draw bridge. In back of him were about one-hundred Knights in fighting armor all in the process of making adjustments to their gear in preparation to leave the Castle and go to war. The King was shaking hands with his Knights and wishing them all good luck and a speedy return. A pat on the back by the King was something to be remembered.

Slide Rule, the King's No. 1 architect and Igor, the King's contractor stood at the King's side to console him.

"I hate going to war," said the King.

"But sometimes it's necessary to bring harmony to the land," said Slide.

"Thank you for understanding, Slide. It is very much appreciated." Slide gives Igor a dirty look knowing he has scored some points for himself and his company, Building Blocks, Inc.

Igor, not to be out done, steps forward. "Your Majesty. If I may suggest, it seems as though this is going to a long and bloody battle. Perhaps there is a way to sit down and reason with the enemy. Maybe a resolution can be worked out. Maybe you can avoid battle."

"Ahaaa, very good Igor. That is why your leadership at Moat Designs, Ltd. is so important to me. Yes, that is good. But, to be honest, I have no intention in engaging in any kind of fighting."

Igor makes a grand gesture to the King's Army of Knights. "Really, then what is this all about, I If I may ask?"

"Tactics. Tactics. Tactics," answered the King.

"Can you be more specific for Slide and I," asked Igor.

21

"Yes, please, that is a good idea. Let's sit down here and I'll tell you my thoughts. My strategy if you will."

As they sat down, large leafed branches were brought over to shield the King, Igor and Slide from the burning sun. Watered down wine was instantly served.

"I'm really quite excited about hearing your battle strategy," said Slide. "Well, let me tell you this in a way that will drive home the significance of what I'm about to do. First of all, Igor, do you have any enemies out there in the business world?"

"Well, yes. But I don't think of them as enemies. Other contractors that I go up against are like an enemy as we must compete. I know all of them, but they are my friends. But when we are competing for the same project, I think of them as my enemy,"

"Very good. How about you Slide? Any enemies?"

"Yes, in the same manner that Igor has spoken of, your Majesty."

"Very well. Good. Now, the next question. Take one of your most fierce competitors. Does he have an enemy?"

Igor thought about this. "Yes. He does have an enemy. A subcontractor felt he should have been allowed a change order and the contractor denied it costing him a lot of money. He really doesn't like him anymore."

"Yes, I see. So, let me see if I have this right. Your enemy has an enemy?"

"Yes, that is correct."

"Is that enemy your friend?"

"Well, no. Not really."

"Wouldn't it be interesting if you were friends?"

22

"Ahaaaa. . . Why?"

"Because, someone once said, *'The enemy of my enemy is my friend.'*"

Slide repeated it slowly. "The enemy of my enemy is my friend."

Igor is all excited. "Wow, I can see that. That is a great way to think about it."

The King takes a sip of his watered down wine and is getting rather happy. "Yes, you see, in business and marketing, companies form strategic alliances with other companies to gain a strategic advantage based upon their offering, or how their services or products work together. If there is a competitor, and there is someone else that is competing against them that is not your direct competitor, then there is a reason for the two companies to work together in some form or informal alliance to gain an advantage."

"How could the sub help me in my business?" asked Igor.

"They could refer their leads to you, and you could give him the work if you get the project."

"Oh, I hadn't thought of that. Good. I like it."

Slide is also getting the message. "So, how does this apply to your situation? You say there is going to be no fighting, but looking at your assembled troops, it looks like this is the big one to me."

"I'm going to use the same strategy. I have directed my troops to march in full uniform to the edge of the field where the King I have a problem with resides. On the other side of the field is going to be a Strategic Alliance of mine, another King, who also is having a problem with that King. When that King sees the size of our armies slowly descending on him, he will eventually call for a truce and then we can sit down and negotiate. See, I will win and there will be no blood spilled on the field of battle."

Where did that expression come from, your Majesty?"

The King 🏰 McKenzie

"The expression goes back hundreds of years and actually is reflected in many ancient cultures. It has been applied in war and in business. It is a good history lesson for all of us."

Relationships are important; strategic relationships are very important.

Note: From Wikipedia, the proverb *"the enemy of my enemy is my friend"* suggests that two parties can or should work together against a common enemy. Although it is often described as an Arabic proverb, there is no evidence of such an origin. The earliest known expression of this concept is found in a Sanskrit treatise on statecraft dating to around the 4th century BC, while the first recorded use of the current English version came in 1884.

STORY #3
Adaptive Reuse, or How to Reinvent Yourself?

THE KING KNOCKED ON THE DOOR of Slide Rule's office. Slide was principal architect of the Castle, and owner of Building Blocks, Inc. Hearing from the inside "go away" the King pulled the rope handle and entered the inner sanctum of Slide's office. In the corner huddled together were Slide and Igor, the owner of Moat Designs, the prime contractor for the Castle.

Slide looks up and now sees the King and immediately wonders if this is his last day as architect for the Castle, or life, for that matter. "My sincere apology. I was so engrossed in our conversation that I didn't bother to see who it was. How can I help you? Here take a seat." Slide turned toward Igor. "Igor, get our King some wine."

"Oh, don't worry about it. You didn't know it was your King and I came quite unannounced."

Igor scrambles and brings grabs a pitcher of watered down wine and mugs. They all settled in.

"So, why the big meeting?" asks the King.

Igor speaks up unafraid of the King. "Your Majesty, Slide is depressed as he has no work, and that worries me, as I need him, for he creates my work."

"Sounds like a monopoly to me," said the King.

"Monopoly?" questions Slide.

The King is in a good mood. "Oh, don't worry about that. Monopoly® might make a good game someday! So, just go out and create yourself some work. Seems pretty easy to me."

"Your Majesty, you just can't create work out of thin air. This is a recession. Everyone has slowed down and everyone is looking for work and they are

25

even lowering their prices just to get cash flow so some of their employees can eat."

"So, reinvent yourself."

"Huh," says Igor.

"Reinvent yourself. Go with the flow. Go with the market. Become an expert in what is needed, not what is not needed."

"I'm going to ask for some help on that one," says Slide. He takes the pitcher or wine and refills up the King's mug.

"Reinvent yourself is to say, become overnight what the market needs. For example, in the present economy there are plenty of abandoned buildings. Some of these are foreclosed distressed properties that are aged and need help. Consider becoming an adaptive reuse specialist. You and Igor could do this together as a team. You approach the real estate brokers and tell them, 'Boy, do I have a deal for you.' And then explain that because of your expertise as an adaptive reuse specialist, you can help them sell their buildings."

"If I may ask, how can we help them do that, your Majesty?"

"It's easy. Since you're the expert at adaptive reuse, you can show them that the abandoned manure station on the busy intersection can actually serve as an excellent location for a new restaurant. Or that the strip shopping center can serve as a small church looking for flexibility and multiple spaces. It's all a matter of perception and you can help the broker get a sale by helping them both see new uses for old buildings."

"How to you get paid?" asked Slide.

"Any astute real estate investor knows that buying the wrong property can cost them a lot of money. You, the architect who is an expert at adaptive reuse, provide them, for a small fee, the necessary planning documents and zoning checks. You provide a schematic site plan, and visit with the city and county and other applicable government bodies to determine feasibility, site restrictions, parking requirements, and other information so the owner can make an educated purchase. Since they're buying an abandoned building that probably needs help, they're getting it far under the market value and saving money. When you can help a person save money, you'll win every time. And when they buy they feel somewhat obligated and indebted to you, so you get the commission to complete the work. Sometimes it's part of the contract. You are their hero."

"I never thought of that," said Slide.

"That's why he is the King," says Igor.

The King, now getting quite happy with all that watered down wine, gets up and makes a wobbly bow toward Igor who is now clearly happy at being recognized by the King.

"Furthermore," said the King. "There are only three buying motives to consider. Someone does something because they're either going to make money, or they're going to save money, or they buy from you because they want to work with you. In this case, as the unabashed expert in adaptive reuse, you satisfy all three of these with the added advantage of also helping the broker get a real estate commission."

Slide is puzzled. "But your Majesty, I have one question. How do you become an adaptive reuse expert?"

"Think back on all of the building projects and particularly renovation projects you've done. There are probably quite a few that qualify as an adaptive reuse project. You just need to market them. Come up with a slogan, such as "I'm an Adaptive Reuse Specialist and I can save you both time and money." Slide repeats the phrase. "I'm an Adaptive Reuse Specialist and I can save you both time and money."

"There you go! Done!"

***Don't be the company whose primary marketing tools are Blinders
preventing them from seeing what's going on around them.
Strategy is about seeing.***

Note: From Wikipedia, **Monopoly** is an American-originated board game
originally published by **Parker Brothers.** Subtitled ***"The Fast-Dealing
Property Trading Game"***, the game is named after the economic concept of
monopoly—the domination of a market by a single entity.

STORY #4
Nothing Changes, Ever

THE KING STANDS IN FRONT OF THE MAKE SHIFT CLASSROOM. He is eager to get started, but Igor, of Moat Designs, the prime contractor for the Castle, has not arrived.

"Your Majesty," said Slide Rule, the King's No. 1 architect and owner of Building Blocks, Inc. "Perhaps we need to postpone your seminar. There's no one here but me."

"Nonsense. It is I who schedules the seminar, and it is I who will give it."

Just then Igor comes running in completely out of breath. "Your Majesty, I'm so sorry I'm late. I ran into some scheduling problems with the new foundations and I had to make sure it was done correctly."

"Nothing changes, does it," said the King who appeared to be a bit agitated about Igor's late arrival.

"I don't think that's true at all." said Igor. He takes a seat and looks around realizing that he and Slide are the only two in the classroom. "Your Majesty, where is everyone else?"

"You're always late," commented the King looking at Igor.

"But for good reason."

"Yes, yes, I've heard it all before. Now, the reason that you two are here, is that you're the leading construction contractors for the Castle and I wanted to conduct a Master Class so I can share my wisdom. When you learn my lessons, you can do even a better job and make more money."

"Excellent," said Slide. He looks at Igor. "We're ready."

"Good. First, take note of this statement. 'Everything is the same and every-

29

thing is different.' What does that mean to you?"

"You must have made a mistake for the sentence contradicts itself," said Igor. "Nonsense. Let me give you an example. The first thing everyone does in the morning is get their coffee and then check their wall to see if anyone wrote on it."

"I'm lost, your Majesty."

"It's partly a future thing you'll understand someday. Now, hundreds of years ago, the first thing that people did when they got up in the morning was to check their wall to see if anyone wrote on it. Right?"

"You're speaking of cave walls, your Majesty?"

"Yes. So, in reality, nothing has changed and everything is different."

Igor and Slide exchanges looks hoping there isn't a test at the end.

"Another example. When you were in school and you misspelled a word, what did the teacher do?"

Silence in the classroom.

"They underlined the word in red. Now I ask you, when someone writes on a computer, what does the computer do when you misspell a word? It underlines it in red. See, everything is different and everything is the same."

"If I may, your Majesty. I don't really understand what you're saying, but assuming I did, how does that help us in business?"

"Slide, an excellent question. Very good Slide."

Slide smiles proudly and looks at Igor who is making faces at him. "Everything the same, and everything is different means there are trends, and these trends repeat themselves. In business it's sometimes referred to as the pendulum effect. What's here today is gone tomorrow, but will return, eventually in a new way."

"I still don't know how to apply it to business to help me make money."

"Okay. Try this out – a long time ago, pioneers had to cook outside, as we do. Then people became civilized, and they cooked inside. Then barbecuing became the new way to cook, so people cooked outside on special occasions while they have a perfectly good stove on the inside. Then people who wanted to barbeque, decided they should barbecue inside so special ranges were designed that include a grill on top to simulate barbecuing."

"Everything is the same, but everything is different. I think I've got it," said Slide.

"It gets worse," said the King. "Some people are now putting brick ovens outside on their patio. To top that, when some people go on vacations, they'll cook around an open campfire."

"I am so confused," Igor said.

"Okay. Let me explain how this can help you. Now, here's the important point; understanding that everything is the same and everything is different means that you must change your marketing message based upon today's strategy. One way to accomplish that is to do a survey of your present clients, your past clients, your prospects and your employees around key business indicators. You take the results of these surveys and compare them to what you think the key business indicators are in your company. What you'll find is you're out of sync with what people think of your company. It's referred to by some as gap marketing. You want to close these gaps with your marketing message and future positioning strategies. The goal is an image that your prospect will identify with your company and the products or services that you market."

"Wow, so times change and when they do, we need to know what has been filtered into society in terms of perception, so we can better adapt to the selling climate based upon needs and wants."

"You got it; everything is the same, and everything is different," said the very happy King.

Your marketing message may change over time; it's part of your strategy to monitor this message and to make sure it reflects who you really are, and what you really do.

STORY #5
The Competitive Advantage Diet

"I HAVE DECIDED TO SHED SOME POUNDS," announced the King of the Castle as he entered the room.

Slide Rule, the No. 1 architect for the King reacted immediately. "My King, I'm so proud of you. What brought this on, if I may ask?"

Just at that time a messenger stepped into the room and stood silently waiting to be summoned the King. "Gentlemen, please have a seat. I need to speak with the messenger and I'll be right back to tell you the complete story."

The King leaves and Igor, the King's No. 1 contractor immediately slugs Slide on the shoulder.

"Why did you hit me? That hurts," Slide responded.

"I hit you because you're an idiot."

Slide rubbed his arm. "Explain please, quickly. The King will return shortly."

"Okay. Try this. Don't encourage the King to go on a diet. If he goes on a diet, that probably means he's going to ask us to go on a diet."

"That's not good. I enjoy the four meals I have everyday. Its part of my life style," stated Slide.

"Here comes the King. He looks happy. Let's tempt him with some really good food and get this diet thing out of his mind."

The King takes a seat and unbuttons his vest for more comfort. "Now gentlemen, where were we? Oh, yes. I was going to tell you all about losing weight. I think you're going to find this so interesting that you too are going to want to be part of this experience. You both could lose a couple of pounds."

Slide and Igor exchange looks of terror.

"But it's an individual decision. No one can tell you to do this as it must come from within, as they say," said the King.

Slide and Igor drew a huge sigh of relief. "Your Majesty, while I admire your decision to lose some weight by going on a diet, I will be the first one to say that you look fit. I'm sure that Igor agrees with this."

Igor nodded his head approving Slide's statement.

Slide continued. "Perhaps we can retire to the eatery across the way to enjoy one last meal, as they say, to celebrate this occasion."

"Nonsense. But first of all, I'm not going on a diet. I'm going to make different food selections. It's like in business; you must make certain selection of the kinds of projects or products you want to be known for so you can increase your competitive advantage. Making different decisions as to what you eat is very much like the competitive advantage concept. It's all about strategy."

"I'll be the first one to admit that I have no idea as to what you're talking about," Igor said.

"It's like this. According to Michael Porter there are three methods for creating a competitive advantage. One is by offering a service at a competitive lower cost, two is by increasing the service one receives, and three is to focus on a very narrow market niche so you are considered the expert."

Igor scratched his head. "I still have no idea what you're talking about. It's making me very hungry. Perhaps we should move across the way and sit and enjoy the day, and perhaps grab a bite to eat."

"Very well," said the King. They all amble over to the eatery, and since it was truly a pleasant day in the Kingdom, they took a seat outside in the shade with a gentle breeze blowing that kept the flies away. Slide whispered in the waiter's ear. A moment later watered down wine was served to all.

"Ahaaa, a little wine is fine for me." He sipped eagerly. "So, to continue, making different food selections is like the third way to increase your competitive advantage. All companies can do this; including companies that produce a product. Even architects and builders can sit back and look at ways to become more competitive"

"Okay. I get that part," said Igor. But what about this diet thing."

"It's not a diet. I simply make different choices in order to improve my health."

"Can you give me an example?" asked Slide.

"Sure. That's easy. In fact this is basically known as the caveman's diet or the hunter-gatherers diet. You eat protein, such as meat, chicken or fish first. Even eggs. And then you eat vegetables, and you preferably eliminate your intake of dairy or sour goat's milk. You limit carbs, but when you do eat them you prefer whole wheat to white pasta breads and potatoes. Fruit is okay but in moderation."

"Sounds terrible said Igor."

As Igor said that, the waiter shows up carrying three platters filled with a slabs of meat, vegetables, mashed potatoes and gravy, mostaccioli, fruit and a loaf of while bread for each of them.

"Our little surprise for you. One more meal before your diet starts," announces Slide.

The King is very happy. "That's so thoughtful, and I want to help you so that you can help me. First, it's not a diet, it's making better selections. So, as King, I want – no I insist – you will join me, and we will all do this together. All we have to do is to pick out the meat and the vegetables, and perhaps a small portion of fruit for desert. We will not eat and enjoy the hot steaming bread with the melted garlic butter that smells so wonderful, nor the garlic mashed potatoes, or my absolute favorite, the baked mostaccioli."

"I have one question, your Majesty" asked Slide.

"And, what is that?"

"Is gravy a vegetable?"

Strategy is about how you choose to deliver your services, the market niches or products you manufacture, and the marketing tactics to get your message to your prospect. Strategy isn't about doing everything; it's about making better selections – so your company can have a competitive advantage diet.

Note: This story is dedicated to Dr. Christy Matusiak, D.C., who I think of every time I eat.

STORY #6
Solutions That Work

THE KING WALKED BACK AND FORTH obviously upset about the Castle addition that was being built. The King, the owner of the Castle, had requested the presence of Igor from Moat Designs Ltd., the moat contractor and all around general contractor, and the architect, Slide Rule of Building Blocks, Inc.

They all looked up at the awkward structure that stood before him. Slide the architect and Igor the contractor tried to make themselves look invisible.

"One of the main problems of cutting edge design solutions is that after ten years or so they tend to stick out as a sore thumb on the humanity of mankind," said the King.

"I take offense at that," said Slide the architect. "That's the Castle I designed for you."

"Slide, why is that stone block box tilted 45 degrees and sitting on its corner?" the King asks.

"Oh, I'm in my angled block box period."

"It doesn't fit into the community?" said the King.

"That was the point of the design." answered Slide who was getting less confident by the minute.

"Igor, why the black tarp?" inquired the King.

"Roof leak." But we'll get it fixed before the next pig roast. Don't worry."

"I do worry," that's why I'm King. "That's my job." The King is now really upset.

"You see these solutions and start to wonder. Where architecture is, where it should be, and where it's going? I'm wondering about your wandering work. What happened to solutions that work?"

"We just get another client," said Igor the contractor.

"I never thought of that," said Slide as he titled his head to see the angled granite block.

"You're both idiots," the King said scornfully. "In today's market, solutions that work can be a differentiator. Making a building fit into the community and making it work are prestigious goals, and one can only get there through leadership and determination; that is what architecture is and should be. Strategic planning, the culture of looking ahead as to what is, and what you want it to be, and when you want it to be, is the platform for survival in an aging market of cubed, angled and tilted type of solutions composed of multiple in-harmonious materials that are designed only for themselves and generally leave people out of it."

"Cubed, angled and tilted?" questioned Slide.

"Big block solution," answered the King. "The buildings that get attention are the large out of scale and out of touch buildings are reviewed in reverence by the architecture guru – the critic. Never are the real solutions of American architecture displayed. There is a time and a place for absurd solutions."

"What do you mean by real solutions," asked Igor. "I thought Slide and I worked on real solutions?"

"No, a Castle is not a real solution. Real solutions are the thousands of architects that provide buildings that fit the community and the budget; that work on multiple levels and don't even leak. This mass of architecture is never seen by the gurus and critics, but is appreciated by the thousands who spend their lives working and living in them. Outside their window, across the street, or in the horizon, is that out of scale award winning building leak."

The King continued at his leisure. "For me, a building that works is better then a building that looks like it should leak. Leadership is about determining and promoting real solutions. Taking the position that a building should fit the community and its surroundings, while at the same time reflect the architecture tradition of relevant design, is by far better than a black block box turned on its side. The real secret of architecture is the real beauty of a building that works. The dirty secret of architecture is that many who are professed to be cutting edge, do so at the detriment of the owner, the King, me, who must now live and suffer the often purely inadequate design."

"Wow," said Igor. Igor and Slide looked at each in utter amazement.

Strategically, if you want to stay in business you must consistently provide real solutions that work everyday in everyway. Occasionally there is a place for a cubed, angled black block naked box, but you must be sure, very sure.

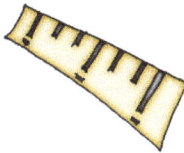

STORY #7
Cardiac Rehab and Business Health

A NEVER ENDING STAIRWAY. At least that's what it felt like as Slide Rule, of Building Blocks, Inc., the architect of record for the Castle, takes step–after–step up the tower stairs with Igor of Moat Designs, Ltd., the builder of the Castle. Finally they reached the top, and stretched out before them was the elevated walkway connecting the towers that surrounded the perimeter of the Castle. It was this defensive position that was manned at all times by the King's Knights in Shining Armor, on the lookout for any invading unfriendly neighbors. The King met his two subjects as they arrived at the top.

"I'm glad that you have both joined me," said the King.

Igor was out of breath and looked for a place to sit down. "Why, your most Honorable Majesty, did we meet you here? It would have been so much easier to meet at the pub over a cold brew of watered down wine as opposed to here at the top of the Castle."

"I have asked you to join me in my cardiac rehab program."

"We did hear that you had an incident a while back, but we did not pry into your health matters."

"That's fine. The doctors diagnosed me with severe aortic stenosis, and after replacing it with a pig's valve, they put me into cardiac rehab."

"A pig's valve?"

"You don't want to go down that road."

"Very well. How long have you been participating?"

"I'm in phase seventeen of their program."

"Phase seventeen? Is that good or bad?"

"I don't know. But I spend a lot of time walking. So, I thought it would be good to walk with my friends, and I immediately thought of you two. I'm sure you're pleased to join me in strengthening my heart."

Igor and Slide look at each other. This was not going to turn out good. They remembered the last time something like this happened when the King went on a diet, and they also went on a diet, by orders of his Majesty.

They started to walk. Slide takes the lead. "So, your Majesty, tell us about your program?"

"It's really quite simple. It's very much like strategic planning. It starts with education, consider it market research, about what is good and what is bad regarding my heart. The goal is to improve my lifestyle in terms of minimizing chest pain, improving diet, improving my exercise program, reducing stress and addressing smoking."

"I can help you with the smoking," said Igor. "You know, I actually visited the cardiac rehab clinic once and I saw a wonderful video that very quickly emphasized the benefits of smoking. It talked about how it helps to cope with anger, stress, and anxiety. Smoking is relaxing and stimulating and a way to be part of a group. It also keeps your weight down, and gives you a feeling of confidence. It also acts as sort of a tranquilizer. As soon as you see the video you have an immediate craving for a cigarette, and I haven't smoked for 30 years."

"I don't think you understand. I'm supposed to stop smoking."

"Oh."

Slide is lagging behind, and the King notices this and turns toward him.

"Slide, what's the problem? Don't you want to help your King? With a little bit of exercise, you might feel better and your business will improve."

"I don't think this walking thing will help improve my business's bottom line at all," replied Slide.

They walked and they talked.

The King continued undaunted by his less then fit friends. "But listen. The cardiac rehab program is a strategic plan for good heart health. It's a process whereby we heart patients are educated as to better ways to live, and as a result, our lives will be better and fuller."

"Can't help me," replied Slide. Igor agreed.

"But it's the same thing as your own strategic plans in your own businesses. As you well know, when it comes down to it, business is really the ultimate game as it has a scorecard, which are the financials, your profit or loss. The cardiac rehab program also has a scorecard, which is set to individual levels of achievement."

"I never thought of it that way," said Igor.

The King continues, as he is excited about his newfound program of good health. "In cardiac rehab you work to improve your scores so that you will be less likely to have a heart incident in the future. The nurses are all there to help you. They are all very attentive and understand your medical issues. In your business, you follow your business plan, which is outlined in a way that is very similar to what they do in cardiac rehab."

"So, if I may," your Majesty, "are you saying that cardiac rehab is similar to a business being successful because they are both seeking to improve one's health in a planned and organized manner."

"Right, you got it."

"I think you're lucky to be involved in such a positive program of health and wealth," said Slide. "If I may suggest something, I think I can actually contribute to your program. I am an expert at stopping to smoke. I can help you with that part of your program."

The King 👑 McKenzie

"Oh Slide. That's wonderful. Excellent. What makes you an expert?"

"I've stopped well over one-hundred times."

Strategic planning is all around you. The reason is, it works.

STORY #8
The Business Cycle

"WHAT A BEAUTIFUL DAY IN THE KINGDOM," said the King to his two friends as they walked along a dusty dirt road leading out to the rural areas surrounding the Castle. Directly behind them were various Knights in Shining Armor on horseback and on foot, sworn to protect their King with their life. Igor, owner of Moat Designs, Ltd. followed along as Slide Rule, the owner of Building Blocks, Inc. the architect for the Castle, talked in an animated voice about the lack of work."

"Business has been so bad that I've had to borrow money against my property," said Slide.

"Why?" asked the King.

"Some people pay and some people don't. I get a project, and then it's not funded. Sometimes I think I'm just not making the right decisions. When my family ran the business long ago it seemed a lot easier."

"That's no big deal," said Igor. "I never know when I've made a good decision."

The King looked at both of them. "I can see clearly now, sounds like a song doesn't it – I think there needs to be a discussion regarding the cycle of business. It's an age old problem, one that has been with us for centuries."

"What do you mean by the cycle of business," asked Slide.

"Okay, while we walk and enjoy this fine day, let me fill you in on some details. First, let me quote, from memory no less, a small paragraph of a book by the famous author James Clavell in his Asian saga *Noble House.* Have either one of you read this fine book?"

Igor and Slide look at each other, and then shook their heads no.

"You really should. It's a book about business in Hong Kong. Take careful note of the sequence of events."

" *'It's the age-old destiny: one-in-ten-thousand coolie (Chinese Worker) strikes gold, harbors money, invests in land, saves money, becomes rich, buys young concubines who use him up quickly. Second generation discontented, spend money, mortgage land to buy face and ladies' favors. Third generation sell land, go bankrupt for same favors. Fourth generation coolie.'* "

"You quoted that from memory? I'm truly impressed," commented Slide.

"But what does it mean?" asked the King.

"I can tell you," said Igor. "It means in the end, you lose."

The King shakes his head. "Let me explain it for you."

As he spoke they arrived at a small stream, and the King waved his hand, and a blanket was immediately provided for them to sit on, and a fresh brew was immediately served.

The King was now comfortable and happy to start another Master Class. "It means that the nature of man is to live from the efforts of previous generations by contributing less, and taking more."

"Actually, that's quite common," said Igor.

"See, it's true, one in ten thousand coolies strike it rich, and the next generation who is brought up with money really doesn't appreciate how it was earned, and thus spends it whimsically. The third generation now is responsible for the business and doesn't have the training or the capacity to manage their business investments, so they start to sell off the assets. And the result, the fourth generation ends up a coolie and the cycle is completed."

"That's a very scary story," said Slide.

"Yes Slide, you're right. It's a terrifying story, but it happens all the time, and will continue to happen to future generations."

"So, what can we do about it?"

"First, it's important to recognize that this business cycle is real, and it can easily happen to any generation. The secret to overcome this situation is long-range planning. It's imperative that businesses plan a minimum of five-to-seven years out. This forces you to step back and look at the big picture."

"So, let me make sure I understand. If you're planning five-to-seven years out, that's not a business plan?"

"Yes. Good for you. We're talking about strategic planning where strategy is determined and set in motion. The business plan implements the strategy."

"Actually that makes a lot of sense," said Slide.

"But here's the real secret. Those companies that use the planning strategies will increase their chances of surviving tenfold."

"What about those companies that don't plan?" asked Igor.

"The cycle of wealth followed by poverty will continue, undaunted by the winds of time," answered the King.

Planning is a management tool that allows you to observe the business cycle and respond to it.

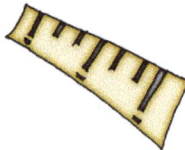

STORY #9
If I Were a Rich Man

THE KING WAS OUT FOR A STROLL and was humming and singing a catchy little tune. "If I were a rich man, Ya ha deedle deedle, bubba bubba deedle deedle dum." Just then he saw Igor, his favorite moat contractor as well as Slide Rule, his favorite architect.

They waved at each other, and then joined up. "I was just enjoying this fine day and I'm glad you're here. I was thinking about a story I would like to tell you."

"That's wonderful," said Igor. "I love your stories."

"What are you fellows up to?" asked the King.

"Well, actually, we're talking about money and how to get more of it," said Slide.

"Perfect. That's exactly what my story is about. Come over here and let's enjoy a brew and I'll tell you my story."

They sat down under the old tree and a very expensive wine was served to them by the King's Servants who had been following discreetly behind.

"This story is worth the very best wine I have in my Kingdom. Cheers!" They all took a sip as the King launched into the story."

"The tale is about two friends; one was a millionaire, and the second one was absolutely flat broke, and in fact, had never had much money in his entire life. Then along came a stranger who gave the broke one a million shillings. So now the two friends were both millionaires."

Slide and Igor looked at each other.

"Time went by and the economy changed, and both the millionaire and the formerly broke person who was also a millionaire both lost all their money. They were then asked what they thought of the fact they were both broke."

"That's a lot of shillings to lose," said Igor.

"Yes, you're right. But listen to their respective responses. The millionaire said, 'I'll be poor and broke until once again I'm a millionaire.' The poor person who had been given the million shillings, and then lost it said, 'I'm poor once again.' "

"That's interesting," said Slide. "The millionaire responded as if he was temporarily out of funds, while the other one's attitude was, I was rich and now out of money, so I'm poor once again"

"Yes, you're right. So, what have you learned?"

"I don't know, but I'll tell you I've been thinking about what it would be like to have a million shillings for a long time."

"The key word is you were thinking of what it would be like to have a million shillings. You didn't picture yourself as a millionaire. You thought of yourself as you are now. What about you Slide?"

"I think it's a bunch of baloney!"

"Okay. Figures. Let's try another way to think about this. Sometimes you have good days, and sometimes you have bad days, right?"

"Yes," they both responded.

"Well, there are always problems, particularly in construction. Something is always going wrong. But my point is, you don't have to let that change how you respond and think about these problems. Even with bad things happening, you can still have a good day. You can have a positive attitude, and it will help you work out the problem. It's the key to strategic thinking."

The King 👑 McKenzie

"I'm having a hard time with this one," said Igor.

"Why is that?" asked the King.

"Because, if it's a bad day, I want everyone to know about it."

"So, you get pleasure by letting everyone know you're having a bad day?"

"Yes."

"You need help!" said the King.

Slide raised his hand as if he was in class. "Your Majesty. If I may, perhaps I can help our friend Igor out."

'Very well Slide. You know Igor better than anyone."

"Very well. In business, where you're dealing with other employees and business associates, it's very much in your best interest to let them know how you're feeling, but it's how you go about it that's important. In fact, just because there's a problem, doesn't mean you should make everyone uncomfortable about it. Strategically, it's much better to be positive, and like the millionaire who is temporarily out of funds, your problems will eventually go away. You'll have also demonstrated your professionalism."

"I think I understand," said Igor.

"Very good. In fact, both of you have always helped me with whatever needed to be done at the Castle. It has pleased me, and now, I would like to present to each of you with a gift of a million shillings. You're both now millionaires."

Both Igor and Slide were so happy they were jumping up and down. Igor was the first one to speak. "How can we thank you?" he said out of breath.

"I was just kidding! Perhaps you can behave as if you're both millionaires and that you're both temporarily out of funds. The money should return to

49

you quite quickly."

**Attitude is the difference between prospering while other
companies struggle constantly.**

NOTE: *"If I Were a Rich Man"* is a popular song from the 1964 musical
Fiddler on the Roof. It was written by Sheldon Harnick and Jerry Bock.

The King ♟ McKenzie

STORY #10
A Different Point of View

THE KING STOOD OUTSIDE HIS CASTLE overlooking his domain. It had been a curious morning as he walked through the Market Square. A Serf had approached him unexpectedly and offered a way to improve the efficiency of the Castle's business, which would enrich the King. He was impressed with the idea, but what really impressed the King is the suggestion had come from a stranger.

A heavily armed Knight stepped forward and whispered in the King's ear, and he nodded his head. A couple of minutes later Igor, the general contractor and moat builder, joined the King followed closely behind by Slide Rule, the chief architect for all of the Castle buildings.

"It's good to see you. Thank you for coming," said the King.

They all stood side-by-side at the end of the drawbridge and viewed the surrounding countryside.

"Thank you for inviting us. Is there any way we can help you?" asked Slide.

"I had an interesting experience today and I thought I might share it with you."

"Please, go ahead," said Igor.

"Well, today, as I was walking through the Market Square, I was approached by one of my subjects. He bowed to me, and I waved to him politely as I passed. Then he stepped forward and said, 'Your Majesty, I wish to speak to you.'"

"Really, that's quite unusual for a commoner to speak without first being spoken to by you, your Majesty."

"Yes, you're right. However, I observed him and he was quite an ordinary

51

fellow and intended no harm. I approached the Serf with two Knights at my side."

"What did he have to say?" said Slide.

"He stated his name was Nor, which I thought was an unusual name. Then he made an interesting observation about the Castle's construction projects."

"Really," said Slide and Igor in unison.

"Yes, he said … 'Your Majesty, I have an observation for you that could help you become more profitable.'"

"I told the Serf to proceed. He stumbled on his words, as he was clearly uncomfortable. 'Your Majesty, you have a lot of different kinds of construction projects going on. If there was one individual that was given a cart with a couple of strong mules with the task of visiting different job sites to pick up tools and equipment, and making a list of what they needed, it would save five-or-six project managers running back to the King's warehouse everyday.'"

"That's a remarkable idea," said Igor.

"Actually, I agree with Igor," said Slide.

"That's the kind of ideas I would expect from the two of you, not a Serf named Nor. But never mind that for now. Let me ask this question, what is it that all companies can learn from Nor's statement?"

Igor and Slide looked at each other lost for words.

"Let me help you. A writer once wrote the following.

'Remember that advice, good advice, comes from unexpected places at unexpected times.'

"That was quoting from Noble House by James Clavell. Have either of you read the book yet? I have mentioned it before."

Slide and Igor shook their head hoping they were not going to be given a homework assignment.

"You should if you're interested about business. But that's for another conversation. What's interesting is the Serf's idea was a very good idea. Many times good ideas can come from people that you don't expect to have a good idea. The reason for their astute observations is they see your business from a different point of view. They see it with their experience, and what they have learned in life."

"I agree," said Igor. "But, I don't get your point."

"Sometimes the best ideas come from someone that pushes the broom at night. Or from the parking lot attendant who innocently comments that 'Ya know, if ya would park the fork lifts over on the other side of the building we wouldn't have so many fumes coming into the office area.'"

"That's very interesting," said Slide.

"It's a really important point. When companies have planning meetings they need to include many different points of view. So invite different people from different departments for part of a meeting. There is a double benefit in that you're communicating that you care about their opinion."

"You know, that makes a lot of sense. I should bring in a project manager from the field to my next meeting. We sit in the office while their world is from the field perspective looking back at us."

"Very good Igor."

"This can also apply to product manufacturers. The people that repair the products in the field would have tremendous insight as to potential changes or even new product ideas."

"Yes, you're right, Igor."

"Your Majesty, I have an observation, if I may?"

"By all means Slide."

"Could it be that all people have value?"

"Very good Slide. Very good."

Care about your employee's opinions, and they will care about your business.

The King

McKenzie

STORY # 11
Differentiation

AT THE ROUND TABLE, everyone was rather tense. The King, who owned the Castle, had requested the presence of the moat contractor, Igor from Moat Designs Ltd., and the architect, Slide Rule, of Building Blocks, Inc.

"I thought you were different," yelled the King. "You're all the same!"

"That's not true," Igor said nervously.

"I agree," said Slide Rule.

"That's the first time my architect and contractor have ever agreed on anything!" The King shot them both a look, and they shut up. The King continued to expound on his wisdom as the contractor and the architect – who just had been squabbling over the depth of the new moat and why it leaked – listened silently. Another Master Class had started.

"Nothing worse than a leaking moat," said the King. "But I should have expected that. Neither of you seem to want to think differently. The regrettable truth is most businesses in a market niche like yours are all alike. They act, sound, market and provide service in exactly the same way. How am I, the King, supposed to tell one company from another? Walk any marketplace and all the vendors look the same. Sit in a presentation and everyone says the same thing. They all claim their work is on time and under budget. Anyone who says that has already lost. They should pack up and go home. Anyone in your business always has to be on time and under budget or you wouldn't be asked to present. No one gets up there and says, 'Well, we miss most of our deadlines and we haven't hit the budget yet, but we're absolutely great designers.' Actually, that might be a refreshing change. But for some companies, they would be telling the truth, but at least they'd get everyone's attention."

"Actually, we do miss our budget most of the time," Igor said.

55

"I know, I know, but that's not the real point. The point is the battle being fought in architecture and construction, and business in general, is about differentiation. How do you make your firm different so you're noticed? How do you show that you offer the services they need, and in fact, are better than your competitors? The answer comes from a concept called Thought Leadership, which occurs when a person or a firm produces innovative ideas that reflect the needs of their clients, and are recognized by their peers and the intellectual community as being perceptive, innovative and timely. Thought leaders also promote those ideas in a variety of ways such as magazine columns, books, presentations, webinars and podcasts. As a result, they inspire others to take action, which ultimately leads to successful strategic positioning."

"Sounds preposterous," said Slide.

"Are you going to fire us?" asked Igor. "I really need this project."

"Keep listening and you might learn something," the King said. "Both of you. In the never-ending struggle to differentiate one firm from another, eventually, someone puts forth a new idea. Since there's never really a new idea, the thought leader generally has a new way of thinking about an old problem. Thought Leadership always revolves around strategic positioning on a number of different levels. It starts with understanding the differences between a strategic plan, a business plan and a marketing plan, and being able to discuss and examine the various levels of tactics relative to position-ing. Surprisingly enough, very few people understand these differences at a tactical and intellectual level."

"You actually believe that stuff," said the moat contractor.

"Yeah, really," said Slide Rule. "Architects don't get into those business angles."

The King glared at them and they both seemed to shrink in their chairs. "That's why I'm King, and you're not. Let me finish. Thought Leadership re-volves around the intellectual discussion of difference. A company that's po-sitioned to do the work is a thought leader just like the company who spends its energy on leading edge design and uses a 'hope the moat doesn't leak' philosophy when they build it. In the end, the company that energetically pursues difference will win more proposals and have happier clients because the substance of their thought is accompanied by their substance of service."

"What are you saying?" asked Igor the moat contractor.

"If your business is going to grow, you need to learn to differentiate yourself from the competition. And you do that by thinking strategically and acting accordingly.

Differentiating is all about what value you provide your client.

STORY #12
Positioning

A LONG TIME AGO, A KING BUILT A CASTLE. To protect himself from their enemies, he had a moat designed by an architect and built by a contractor. The moat surrounded the Castle offering perfect protection with an innovative drawbridge that could be hoisted up completely isolating the King and his people. The King was happy with his architect, Slide Rule of Building Block, Inc., and his contractor, Igor of Moat Designs, Ltd.

One day, the King and his people were attacked. Under a barrage of arrows, the fierce enemy moved into position a large flat surface made of heavy timbers that they carefully lowered into place creating their own bridge. Now, as they could get close to the Castle, they dislodged the gateway, and entered into the heart of the kingdom creating a mighty fight of utterly brave and foolish men only to withdraw in retreat.

The King, who is now quite nervous, called Igor, the moat builder and complained about the attack.

"Why were they able to get in," yelled the King.

"It wasn't my fault," said the moat builder. "It was Slide the architect who designed it."

"Slide," yelled the King, and he instantly appeared.

"It wasn't my fault that you were attacked," countered the architect.

"You're fired," said the King. "Both of you."

Igor and Slide looked very unhappy and glared at each other.

"Wait a minute. I can't fire you. It'll cost too much to replace you."

Igor and Slide now looked very happy and were the best of buddies.

"Okay, now, you both get the lecture," said the King. "You are both very lucky that you're the architect and contractor of record. Otherwise, you would be history as you are not well positioned." A Master Class had started.

"We are here to serve," ventured Slide the architect with a slight bow.

"Yes, very well put," said Igor the contractor. He also bowed to the King, but with more flare and meaning.

The King ignored the comments, bows and the looks. You may think you're well positioned, but you're not. It's truly a miracle you're still both in business," said the King.

"What's this positioning concept?" asked Igor.

"Positioning is the heart and soul of competitive strategies. To be truly competitive, you must be well positioned and you must communicate your ideas through a variety of marketing tactics, and as a result, inspire others to take action by contacting you for your services."

The all knowing King continued. "The only reason there is competition is that you're not satisfying all of the needs of your marketplace, thereby creating opportunities for someone to offer their services to this niche, and eventually they get around to offering their services to your clients. Basically, competition cannot be avoided."

"But, from an intellectual viewpoint, there should be no reason to hire someone else, if you've done your job properly. Your corporate story should be more then 'We did this, and this, and then we did that, and oh, we also did this.' Your story should reflect your prospects and their needs, while at the same time, developing your competitor's weaknesses as your strengths. The prospect should see your company as an integral part of their company. This is the one competitive strategy that is not understood, and therefore not used by most as they just want to get the RFP or RFQ off of their desk."

Igor and Slide don't say a thing as they have no idea as to what is going on and no clue what an RFP or RFQ was about.

The King continued. "The difference is that it's not about you; it's about your customer, me, and the value you bring to my Roundtable. A competitive strategy should leave no doubt that you're becoming part of my team; that you are there to serve me, for I am King."

"Oh, I get it," said Igor. "It's not about the moat; it's all about the value that you, the King will receive, when you select me as your moat contractor."

"Yes, you got it," said the King.

To position your company well is to provide true and meaningful value as part of your service that goes beyond price and budget.

STORY #13
Understanding The Big Picture

IT WAS A SERIOUS DISCUSSION. The King, Igor and Slide were walking through the classrooms which were located in the central part of the Castle.

"I think we should leave them exactly like they are," said Igor.

"I agree," said Slide. Slide and Igor beamed at each other as it was a rare occasion that they were on the same side.

Igor was from Moat Designs, Ltd. and was the all around general contractor. Slide Rule was from Building Blocks, Inc. and was the architect of the Castle. They both worked for the owner of the Castle, The King.

"I think you're both wrong," exclaimed the King.

"But why? A school is a school. So they need a little work. Part of my job is to advise you on how to keep facility expenses low. It's getting tougher-and-tougher to do the work within your yearly budget." said Igor. "I'm suggesting this out of professional courtesy. I could easily say we need to work on this immediately, and I'll make more money."

The three exited the classrooms. "Okay. Let me tell you why. Let's sit over here in the shade and discuss this."

They moved over to the side in front of the school classrooms which were a bit on the shabby side.

"Let me ask you a question," proffered the King. "What is the future of this Castle?"

"That's easy," said Igor. "The future of any Castle is the strong walls that provide a barrier from attacking intruders. That is the only concern that is important."

"Who mans those battlements and who's there to lead them when we're attacked?"

"It's our warriors and our Knights in Shining Armor who fight and lead our battles. It's truly the backbone of our Castle. Without them, we have nothing."

"Good. Excellent! Would you say that we need good warriors and good Knights?"

Igor spoke up again confident that his answers were making a strong impression on his King. "We need the best Knights and the best warriors that we can produce."

"We need the best," said the King repeating Igor's comment. "How do we get the best?"

"We train them to be the very best?"

"Uh, oh," said Slide.

Igor turns to Slide. "What was that all about? You're supporting me on this."

"Not any more."

"I know I'm right." Igor said stubbornly.

"Slide, why don't you tell them what you now understand?" said the King.

"I'll be honored. If we're to have the best warriors and Knights we must train them. In order to do this, we must provide them the very best education from the first day they enter our classrooms to when they graduate."

Igor is getting defensive and his voice is a little hostile. "I agree, but a classroom is a classroom. It is what it is. I do not see the connection."

"Let me take it from here," said the King. "First, it has been established for a long time that there is a relationship between a school facility and the behavior and performance of the student. The school facility can actually contribute to the educational process. As a matter of fact, this is also applied to office buildings and even places like Starbucks® whose environment can increase repetitive returns by how they handle the interior."

Starbucks®?" Slide asks.

"We'll talk about Starbucks® later," answered the King as he continued. "When these planning concepts are applied to the educational setting there is a direct correlation and improvement as the students learn more and want to learn more. Such factors as building age, condition, quality of maintenance, air quality, noise, light, and color, all affect student health, safety and general overall desire to return and learn more."

"Oh," says Igor.

"So let me ask this question. If we want better Knights, what must we do?"

Slide speaks up. "We must improve the quality of the learning environment so that the school produces the best of the best. And that means we will have the smartest warriors and the smartest Knights in Shining Armor."

"Yes, you are exactly right, the King says. "And it also means that our ability to make better pottery, clothes, and crafts, and to prepare food, to name a few, will also be improved, all just because we took some time to take care of our educational facilities. It's a lesson for everyone, including the contractor, architect, businessman and politician, all who should always be looking at ways to train their staff."

"I now also agree with you," said Igor. Slide nods his head.

"Igor," said the King. "What are you now going to do?"

"I need to work on our schools immediately," replies Igor.

"Good, and next week, I'm sending you both to a training class. I want the best staff possible."

Training your staff is a critical strategic tactic.

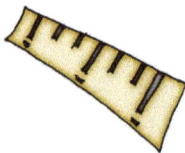

STORY #14
Becoming Comfortable

THE KING, IGOR AND SLIDE WERE OUT WALKING along a river that ran adjacent to the Castle. Slide Rule of Building Blocks, Inc. was the head architect and Igor, from Moat Designs, Ltd. was the general contractor. Behind them walked a small army of Knights, warriors and servants ready to defend or make the King comfortable in any way they could. Flanking them on all sides were other teams of Knights watching out for any danger that could approach their King.

"What a wonderful day. Let's sit over here on this river bank and enjoy the view," said the King.

They all sat down and the entourage immediately started to approach the King, but the King waved them off.

Slide kept squirming around. "This is not very comfortable, your Majesty."

"Do you have to be comfortable to enjoy the surroundings?" asked the King sitting back and looking quite refreshed and content. "Just look. This is the river that provides us with fresh water."

Igor who is also squirming on the ground trying to find a comfortable spot. "Your Majesty, with all due respect, with all of your responsibilities, you should be comfortable at all times. With a wave of your hand you could have the servants bring to us the soft blankets they are carrying just for this purpose."

The King ignored Slides comment. "So, let me ask both of you a question. What is the best way to grow your business?"

"That's impossible to answer. There are so many things that impact the growth of a business. It really is a lot of ideas and concepts that are networked together," answered Slide.

"Igor, how about you?"

"I agree with Slide. There is no one answer to the question as each and every business is different."

"Do you know how I became King, Slide?"

"Ahaaa, that's a tricky question. I think you were born into it."

"Really, is that what you think?"

"No."

"Well, let's not pursue that point." Slide looks enormously relived. "I became King because I put myself in uncomfortable situations, and learned from them. You can't learn anything by sitting in a glass office all day where everything is status quo. Then you just exist. Nothing is happening. Oh, you might respond to a competitor in some unusual way, but everything is pretty much the same."

"So you're saying we have to be uncomfortable to get ahead so we can be comfortable?"

"Yes. That's what I'm saying."

Igor is still squirming on the ground clearly not enjoying the beautiful view of the river and the fields behind it. "If I may say so, isn't that a bit weird?"

"The only way to become successful is to learn. In order to learn you must reach out to new material and experiences that might make you uncomfortable learning, but it will, in the end, all come together to help you. It's this process of being uncomfortable that actually helps you grow."

Igor is thinking. "Well, come to think of it, I was building a small hut just to the right of the Castle and I ran into a construction problem. It was an issue dealing with the structure and I had always solved the problem in the conventional manner. But I decided to explore, to reach out if you will, to other builders. It was very uncomfortable asking those questions, but soon enough I had the answer, a new answer that made my building better. And as a result of experiencing that uncomfortable period, I actually became a better builder."

"Yes, that's it. Good for you!"

You must become comfortable with being uncomfortable.

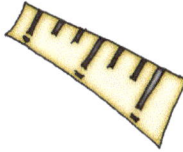

STORY #15
Sour Grapes

"I TOLD THEM THEY'RE MAKING A MISTAKE," stated Slide Rule owner of Building Blocks, Inc., the No. 1 architect working on the Castle grounds.

"How so?" asked the all-knowing King.

"I told them they selected the wrong architect. I'm far better than the firm they selected, and on top of that, my price is competitive."

The King, who was sitting back in his throne quite comfortably, said "So, you're telling me you told your prospect they made a bad decision?"

"Yup, that's what I did and I'm happy I did it."

"I would have never done that," stated Igor, owner of Moat Designs, Ltd., a general contractor.

"Good for you Igor," said the King.

"Uh, Oh," said Slide.

"Uh, Oh," is right said the King. "You made a really big mistake."

"But I didn't get the job. I was a perfect fit for it, and I was trying to communicate to the owner that they're going to have problems. I could have saved them a lot of money."

The King got up from his throne. "Let's take a walk and talk this out." Another Master Class had started.

The two fell in step with the King with Igor making smirky faces at Slide Rule.

"Don't worry," said the King. "Even though you made the mistake, it's okay. It's one of the most common mistakes made by managers."

"How so?" asked Slide.

"Never, ever, say anything bad about a prospect or a competitor, as it will come back to haunt you. It's the worst thing you can do."

"Why not? I've lost them."

"But there's always the future. Expressing sour grapes might make you feel better, but it harms your reputation."

"I had sour grapes for dinner last night. I feel quite alright," said Slide.

"Slide, you're an idiot. Let's review what sour grapes actually means. The expression alludes to the Greek writer Aesop's famous fable about a fox that cannot reach some grapes on a high vine, so the fox announces they are sour."

"If I may, your Majesty. I think you've been enjoying a little bit too much wine," stated Igor.

The King gives Igor the look, and continues on never missing a beat. "Sour grapes is an expression of the loser's scorn for something that didn't go their way. By expressing sour grapes you are insulting them and that means you're only damaging yourself in the long run."

"If I insulted them, then I'm truly happy," said Slide Rule.

"You're missing the point. By expressing sour grapes, you hurt yourself more than any feelings you could hurt of your intended target."

"How so?" asked Igor as the exited the Castle and walked toward the Moat Bridge in the brilliant sunlight.

"It's easy. It means that if you say something bad about someone else, they're going to wonder, if I get into a relationship with them, and something goes wrong, then they're going to be saying bad things about me. Then they make the conclusion, that the last thing I need is a company promoting disrespect about me or my company. That isn't the company I want to work with, let alone be tied in someway financially."

"Wow, all of that? I hadn't thought about it that way," responded Slide who is now sulking in his misery.

"So, if I may say, your Majesty, what Slide has done is actually hurt the image of his company, and his brand, if you will, with his disparaging remarks. Should he apologize?"

"Yes. But you have to be careful because it can actually get worse. Did you speak to him in front of anyone?"

"Why yes, some of my employees were there, as well as some of his employees."

"Now, you're in real trouble," stated Igor.

They arrived at the Moat and walked out and stood in the middle of the bridge. "Your employees are now repeating what you said, and to make it even more complicated, your prospect's employees are doing the same thing about you."

"What should I do now?"

"It's like this moat. The water doesn't move. It just sits here. What you have created is a stream which branches off to other streams. It just keeps going and going. You need to get a meeting with the prospect, and make an offer to help him in some way. You must tell them that you value their business, and even though it didn't work out this time, you would like to continue to develop the relationship."

"What you're saying is I need to build a dam."

"Now you understand. All business must build dams from time-to-time. This is your time."

It's hard to lose, but you must do it with pride coupled with a positive attitude, and if you do, the prospect will remember you.

STORY #16
Suspect or Prospect?

"WHAT TO DO? WHAT TO DO? WHAT TO DO?" said Igor of Moat Designs, Ltd. the builder of the Castle.

The King looks up from his parchment tablet. "What to do?" he commented "Sit down with me in front of this magnificent roaring fire. I'm taking time from my busy schedule to relax."

"I have all of these new leads for construction work, and I've no way to tell which one is good, and which one is bad. If I call all of them it'll take forever."

Slide Rule, of Building Blocks, Inc., the architect of record for the Castle walks in and overhears the conversation. "Why don't you give them to me?" Igor shoots him a look.

Slide smiles. "Just thought I'd ask. If they need construction services, they might need some design work."

"Why don't you gumshoe it?" exclaimed the King.

"Gumshoe! What's that?" asked Igor.

"You don't know what a gumshoe is?"

Igor and Slide look at each other and shake their head.

"This is a future thing. In around 1900 the word "gumshoe" became known for a detective and alludes to the fact that they spent a lot of time checking out clues, and they did that by walking. They wore rubber soled shoes to make it easier. Hence, the name gumshoe."

"So, how does that apply to us?" asked Igor.

The King 🪑 McKenzie

"Another Master Class is now in session. Do you see any parallel to what a private detective does, compared to what a business developer does?" questioned the King.

Slide steps forward. "If I may say, your Majesty, you've been reading far too many cheap pulp fiction detective novels."

"I'm very serious here. And besides, some of those detective fiction novels are actually quite well done. For example, read *Coyote Trap,* the second novel in the *Fargo Blue Detective Series." (shameless self–promotion).*

"So be it. But how can a detective help us?"

"If I may ask, don't you spend a lot of time checking out leads?" asked the King.

"Sure, that's where we get our business," answered Igor.

"Isn't that what a detective does when they're working on a case. Don't they check out leads?"

"Never thought about it, but yes, they do. Does that mean we're private detectives?"

"In a way, yes. But let's take it a step further. What do private investigators do that you don't do?"

Igor and Slide look at each other.

"The answer is, they work the case. They ask questions, and then more questions. There's a lot you could be doing to learn more about a prospect. Are they a suspect or a prospect? Do they really have a need, a need that requires a your services? Asking question is very strategic and can help you save time and money."

"That makes some sense. How do we learn more?"

73

"Now that's a great question, and the answer is to ask more questions. You need to learn more about your prospect. If they are a prospect, are they an "A" prospect, a "B" prospect or a "C" prospect? Like the detective, you need to get out into the field and to start to examine everything that surrounds the prospect."

Slide walks over, opens the door and looks at the field outside the Castle walls.

"No, you dummy. It's an expression for getting out of your office. You can talk to the people that surround the suspect, that know them the best. You can go to different trade-shows and talk to them there. You must become knowledgeable about their business goals, and about their particular problems. If you help them solve a business issue with your services, you'll be a hero and you'll get business."

"Sounds like a lot of work."

"It's a lot of work. And eventually you must actually talk to the prospect in person."

"Never," said Slide.

"Me neither. That's completely out of the question."

"Why?"

They look at each other. They have nothing.

"Well, as homework (groans), you're going to go out into the field and you're going to start to pretend that you're a detective, and you're going to look for clues to solve your case. You case is to work the clues to get business."

"And if we don't," challenged Slide.

"Oh, that's easy. I'll go out and find a real detective and I'll ask him to locate a real architect and a real contractor that can take over your responsibilities."

74

The King 🪑 McKenzie

"Oh my," said Igor. "I think that becoming a detective might be an interesting experience. What do you say, Slide?"

"Lead me to the lead."

Become a detective and investigate by asking questions.

STORY #17
The Seasons of Psychology

"I'M DEPRESSED," said Igor as he slumped down in the chair in front of the King.

Slide Rule, the chief architect for the Castle and owner of Building Blocks, Inc. looked at Igor, and then at the King. "Igor, you shouldn't act that way in front of the King. He could throw you in the dungeon."

"The way I feel, that would be a good thing," said Igor, owner of Moat Designs, who was the primary moat builder for the King.

"I offer free room and board," replied the King.

"That's exactly what I'm looking for," said Igor.

". . . in exchange for hard labor."

"Oh!"

"How about if we all go for a walk," suggested the King.

"Not me. It's all overcast, and foggy. Can't see anything."

"Igor, shouldn't you be building a moat or something?" asked Slide.

"What's the point? Build them and bill them and then beat them up for payment."

"This time of year is always difficult for a lot of people," said the King.

"How so?" asked Slide.

Slide moves over to his friend and puts his hand on his shoulder. "Igor, let's sit over here and listen to what the King has to say."

"Sure. Why not?" Nothing to lose, and nothing to gain."

"Is this another one of those Master Classes?" asks Igor. They both take a seat and the King starts to pace.

"Yes. It will help you. Just settle yourself and become comfortable. I want to talk a bit about the ups-and-downs that people and businesses face on a continual basis."

"Businesses get depressed?" asked Slide.

"Yes. In a way, you're right. Many businesses go through slumps similar to what people experience. Remember, its people that run the business, and if some people are not in top form, then the business suffers."

"That's a good point," said Slide.

"You may find this interesting. A major impact on how people feel actually has to do with the weather."

"You're kidding," said Igor. "I'm really depressed and you want to talk about the weather?"

"Just let him go on," said Slide.

"Think about how you feel. As the days get shorter and colder, you feel closed in. Eventually it's dark, cold and icy in the morning when you go to work, and when you travel home, it's the same way."

"I hate it when it's dark outside. In fact, it's really tough for contractors as their working hours are shorter. In fact it can really cut into productivity issues, which means less billings," said Slide.

"I'm getting depressed again," said Igor.

"Let me continue," said the King. "Then all of a sudden the air feels different, and it slowly becomes lighter outside. Spring is starting to reveal itself, and it puts a spring into your step."

"So, bottom-line. What are you saying?" asks Slide.

"There's more. Listen to this, the seasons of the year impact people on how they think and behave. When the holiday season passes, some people begin to feel alone, because they are alone, or they are in a relationship where they feel they are alone. Spring brings new energy to people, and daylight saving starts which also helps people with their mood, while summer brings out feelings of wanting to do something, to get their lives going in the right direction, or what they think is the right direction. They take action. Fall is a season of rest and of remembering and then the process starts over again."

"Wow, that's impressive," said Slide.

"I refer to these changes as The Seasons of Psychology."

"The Seasons of Psychology? It sounds like a research paper for a doctorial program."

"No, it's in a draft of a novel I read."

"Who wrote it?"

"This novelist I know." *(shameless self-promotion).*

"You're kidding?"

"No. I'm serious. As business in the future becomes more complicated, psychologists are going to play a bigger and bigger role in educating business leaders about people, and the importance in understanding their employees, and encouraging them to develop programs that say, 'We take interest in you as a person, and we are here to help.' "

"So, it's all about the people?" asked Slide.

"Yes, you must pay attention to people. You must help them up when they're down, you must show empathy to their worries, and you must challenge them to exceed."

"Well said," replied Igor. "Well said."

Remember, its people that grow your business.

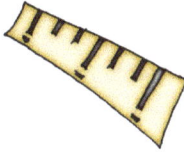

The King 🪑 McKenzie

STORY #18
Does Your Business Need Glasses?

THE KING WAS SITTING BY HIMSELF in the Market Square having just made an inspection of his Castle. A cold brew was served to him, and as he sat there, the warmth of the day felt good. The King's Knights in Shining Armor stood close by, ready to serve their King.

The King glanced around and assures himself that no one was watching him, so he pulled out a pair of wire frame almost not-yet-invented spectacles and slipped them on so he could read.

Shortly afterward from above came a loud echoing voice, "Hi your Majesty."

The King looked up and saw Igor, the general contractor and head moat builder for the Castle, along with Slide Rule the Castle's architect, who were both leaning over a high stone tower above him and were frantically waving. He could see Igor point to his eyes and mock his glasses, and the somewhat embarrassed King quickly removed his spectacles and waved back.

"We'll be right with you," Slide yelled.

It didn't take long before the two arrived and joined their King, and they were also served cold brews.

"Your Majesty, I must ask you, were you wearing glasses?" asked Slide.

Igor and Slide started to laugh and then stopped immediately when they realized the King was not laughing with them.

The King reached into his dark red velvet robe, and took out his glasses and puts them on. "Slide, you wear glasses. Why are you making fun of me because I was also wearing them?"

"It was Igor, your Majesty." Igor slugs Slide in his arm.

80

Slide acts as if he's been mortally wounded.

The King ignores them both and takes off his glasses and looks at them. "You know, these glasses actually represent an important business planning concept."

"Really?" said Slide.

"Is it about cheating?" asked Igor who immediately broke into laughter. Slide also started to laugh, and then they both stopped as the King was glaring at them.

Slide cleared his throat in an effort to be more considerate. "How do your glasses represent a business planning concept?"

"I'm sure you're aware that the last seven years have been tough from an economic point of view. Many businesses have disappeared or have gone broke. Let me ask you a question, why in almost any given market niche do some companies remain in business, and other ones go broke?"

Slide and Igor exchange looks, both knowing it's a trick question. "I don't know," Slide answered.

"Neither do I," said Igor.

The King started to get up and pace. A Master Class was in session. "Well first and foremost, it's about vision."

"Really," responded Slide. "Vision?"

"Yes. You see, when there's a change in buying patterns such as a slow economy, for whatever reason, those with vision have survived."

"What does that mean?" Igor said.

"Vision is strategic."

81

"Exactly what I was going to say," said Slide.

The King stops, turns and walks over and stands in front of Slide. "Really?"

Slide knows he's been called out on the cobblestone. "No, your Majesty."

"Right." The King continues to pace. "Please understand that vision is the responsibility of the CEO, who worries about the future positioning of the company – basically the ability to compete with the right products or the right services."

"Really," said Igor. "I had never thought of that."

"Of course you haven't. It's vision that lets you survive this year, the next year, the next five years, the next ten years and it's vision that makes you a force to be reckoned with in your market niche."

"It's starting to make sense," responded Slide.

"Good for you Slide. See, you've heard of companies that have reinvented themselves. What they're doing is adjusting their vision to fit the current market as well as their future market, or new markets, by making adjustments, such as distribution, product delivery, purchase, terms, or the services they offer, or even the products themselves. It's these companies that are the heroes of the business world. They're constantly examining their vision."

"That makes perfectly good sense," said Igor.

"See, all the manufacturers of buggy whips will someday go out of business when buggies go away, but if those same manufacturers' vision could see themselves as part of the transportation industry, then they would still be in business many years from now."

Slide and Igor exchange glances.

"Now, I have a question for you; do your respective companies need glasses?"

Igor looked puzzled. You mean, do we need to re-examine our vision so we can make sure we're a viable company in the marketplace for years to come?"

"Yes. Very good Igor, very good. You have once again listened to what I've said, and once again I'm going to save you from the gallows."

Slide faints.

The King roars in laughter.

Consider subcontracting companies that offer different trades and promote Sole-Source of Responsibility eliminating conflict between trades and the resulting finger pointing. What vision can you create with your team that provides more value than your competitor?

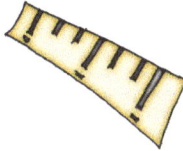

The King 🪑 McKenzie

The King ♚ McKenzie

PART II
BUSINESS PLANNING

The business plan says, based upon the strategic plan, this is what we're all going to do this year to work toward accomplishing the strategic plan. The implementation of the plan is much more detailed, and can be used as a basis for performance reviews. A business plan, used properly is a management tool – it's meant to be used throughout the year as a guide for managing the business. The plan includes one-year proforma financials ideally on a month-by-month basis.

THE BUSINESS PATH TO GROWTH AND PROFIT

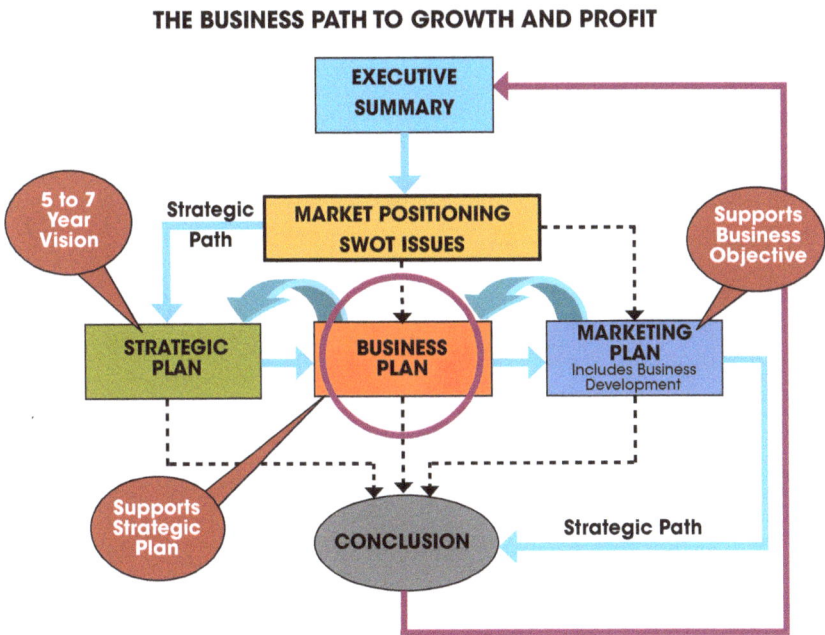

Fig. 2 The Business Planning Process - Business Plan

85

STORY #19
The King's Crop Fails

THE LAND WAS BARREN AND DRY, and becoming a dust bowl.

"Your Majesty, I'm so sorry this has happened to you," said Slide Rule, the King's No. 1 architect as he stood with his King.

"My sentiments exactly," said Igor, of Moat Designs, the contractor for the Castle.

Slide, the King and Igor stood there side-by-side looking over a vast waste-land of raw hard and unturned earth. Little chimneys of dust circled violently and then quickly dissipated. They all turned and headed back toward the Market Square.

"This is a problem, but then again, it isn't a problem," said the King.

"Why is that," asked Slide.

"I knew it was coming," stated the King.

"But no one knows that, not even modern TV weather channels can know that," commented Slide.

"Very good Slide," the King said commenting on the knowledge that Slide had of the future. "But I knew that the crop would fail."

Igor was very puzzled by this TV thing. "How did you know, your Majesty?"

"For thousands of years, sooner or later, the crop fails."

"Wow. Are you saying that no matter what, over time, sooner or later, the crop is going to fail, and that's a sure bet?"

"Yes. And it also means that your business will fail Igor, and yours too Slide."

86

Slide waved his hand through the air. "No, that can't happen to me. I'm in good shape."

"Think about what I just said. For thousands of years, sooner or later, the crop fails."

"You mean, it's going to happen, we just don't know when?" questioned Igor. "Right. And that means I have stored extra grain in case of an emergency. Both of you should also have a backup plan for your business."

"How can I possibly do that?" Slide said.

Igor takes a seat at the table in the Market Square. "If it's thousands of years, I have nothing to worry about. I'm only going to last another thirty or forty years."

The King also sits down. "It's time for another Master Class. What I'm saying is, sooner or later it's going to happen. The economy will fail and then you'll be in trouble."

"Can't get much worse than it is now," said Slide taking a seat.

"So, what's the solution?" said Igor.

"Napoleon Bonaparte," responded the King.

"Really! Wasn't he the famous military General who became the Emperor of France?

"Yes, said the King. "He was a superb military strategist. You must understand that business is similar to warfare, as there are many common elements. Napoleon was famous for his ability to maneuver. Consider the following."

"Napoleon's power to adjust and maneuver on the run was based in his novel way of planning. First he spent days studying maps and using them to make a detailed analysis. A plan was developed. Then he calculated contingencies: if the enemy did x, how would he respond? If part

of his plan misfired, how would he recover? The plan was fluid and gave him so many options, that he could adapt it indefinably to whatever situation developed. He had anticipated so many potential possible problems that he could come up with rapid answers to any of them."

"So, if I may apply what you just stated, businesses must be able to maneuver; they must be able to look at the big picture and adjust to coming market conditions," stated Slide.

"But I think there's more," said Igor. "I think the King is saying, you must have built in contingencies in your business so you can react before your competition figures it out."

"Very good Igor. I'm pleased with both of you. But there's one more part of this that is critical."

"Understand, in life as in war, nothing ever happens just as you expect it to."

The King smiled. "It means you must constantly plan for every contingency. That's what Napoleon Bonaparte did."

"You know, your Majesty, when you talk I can only think of one thing," said Slide.

"What's that?"

"My company business plan."

"Good Slide. Very good."

Do you have a "What If" section in your business plan?

Quotations are from Robert Greene's *"33 Strategies of War,"* published by Penguin Books.

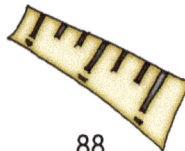

STORY #20
The Economy

BUSINESS WAS NOT LOOKING TOO GOOD IN THE KINGDOM. The Castle, built by Igor of Moat Designs, Ltd. and designed by architect Slide Rule of Building Block, Inc., opened its drawbridge every morning in anticipation of the King's subjects making the trek in to sell their goods to the townspeople. Now only a handful of serfs, farmers and craftsman made their way over the drawbridge and through the gates.

The King, Slide Rule and Igor were discussing the problem of the dwindling economy.

"Why aren't the people coming in like they used to?" asked Slide. "We need their grains and wares more then ever."

"Do you have money to pay for them?" answered the King.

"No. I must barter and chew them down and settle for less."

"Then, that's your answer."

Igor was pacing back and forth. "I'm in real trouble. The housing market has crashed. My contracts are being cancelled and even when I squeeze my subs for more margin, I can't get it. The subs are asking me to pay for work performed and I'm over extended at the bank. I'm going to default on my loan real soon. I want to extend the terms with the subs so I can finish the houses and get them to market. But even if I do that, houses are not selling, so I won't get paid. I'm in real trouble."

"You haven't paid me my fee yet," muttered Slide. He was getting edgy realizing now that he might not get paid. He needed the money really bad.

"Quiet, both of you. Listen, you can't even file bankruptcy."

"Bankruptcy?" questioned Slide Rule and Igor in one voice.

"It's a future thing. Here, listen to me, your King."

They sat down and now the King stood before them. A Master Class had just started.

"First. It's not entirely your fault. There were many factors that created this problem. You both had some pretty good years in the past and built a lot of housing. That inventory will have to be absorbed before the market will turn around. More people have less money. Firewood is becoming scarce. Even the cost of maintaining my Knights in Arms is increasing. The cost of steel to make swords has skyrocketed. Also, many farmers and craftspeople have picked up and moved on contributing to the lower output, which adds to the problem."

"Man, I'm depressed," said Igor as he got up and started to pace back and forth.

"Basically, the end of the year will feel better then the beginning of the year. It will feel recessionary, but it will technically not be a full blown recession."

Slide Rule really didn't understand all of this stuff. "So, what's the solution?"

"Time and money."

"Time and money? Tell me more. To me, that's what caused the problem."

"Well, it's going to take time for the economy to make a shift where consumer spending increases. When this happens, the workers that have been laid off will slowly start to be hired. The economy needs to balance itself as it is subject to supply and demand. As the supply of vacant houses is absorbed, then slowly the building market will come back. As it does, farmers will feel more confident and they will invest in the future that once before they took for granted."

"Wow. You're so deep," Slide said as he got up and started to pace back and forth.

"Furthermore, I'm going to initiate a planning event."

"What is that may I ask?"

Now the King started to pace back and forth along with Igor and Slide. "The think tanks at Harvard and other prestigious organizations charted with Thought Leadership say that putting money into the hands of people that will spend it today will stimulate the economy. Those that receive it will invest in their business and the money will circulate, and eventually the economy will be thriving again."

There was a pause in the King's speech as Igor and Slide absorbed the information.

"The King continued. "I have a question for both of you. What have you learned as architects and builders that will help you in the future?"

Igor and Slide looked at each other and were unable to respond to the King's request.

"The answer is one of foresight. Being in business means you must not only think about today. Yesterday is done, but it holds the key to the future. You must always step back and be mindful of what is happening in the global economy that can impact your business. When you see a change, and hopefully before you see a change, you must take steps to protect your investments. You must sit and think and ponder and try and predict what part of the market you should be in if the downturn happens. This is the essence of business planning that everyone forgets about. A business plan is not a report sitting on a shelf. It's a management tool."

The King continued. "You must prepare yourself for the future. Answers might be diversification, new markets, controlling overhead, employee recognition programs, expanded business development and marketing, acquisition, internal cost savings, increased internal communications, establishing stronger alliances with your key business relationships, to name a few. If you had done this, you wouldn't be in the predicament you're both in today."

Igor turned around and looked at Slide, who had his head down, walking behind the King, listening to what he was saying.

"Business planning is the difference between some companies being successful, and other companies going out of business. Business planning allows you to react the market with intelligence."

Igor stopped pacing. "My, you are a good King."

A good plan is the result of the thinking of many people focused on solving a problem and taking steps to implement.

STORY #21
The Right Way

KING WAS RESTLESS and paced back and forth on top of one of the prominent watch towers used when an enemy approached. Slide Rule the King's No. 1 architect and owner of Building Blocks, Inc. paced right behind him. Following Slide was Igor, the No. 1 contractor of the Castle and owner of Moat Designs.

"So, your Majesty, why are we pacing like this back and forth?" said Igor who was a bit out of shape and getting annoyed at the constant back and forth pacing.

"I'm worried about the future. I am worried about making the right decision. I am worried about being worried."

Slide, sensing that he and Igor must bolster their King's spirits in some way to get him out of the dungeon, sort of speak, decided to confront the King. He placed his hand on the King's shoulder and stopped him. "Your Majesty, perhaps making a decision is better than making no decision."

"Oh no. That is clearly wrong. I am the King of this Castle and I must make the right decision. Just any decision will not do."

"But, who is to say it is right or it is wrong?"

The King sat down on part of the stone parapet. "Let me tell you a story that happened a long, long time ago. A company, a very large company, was experiencing drastic changes in their sales of all their products. The company was impacted by the same kind of structural recession that we're experiencing now. The CEO, being proactive, made a statement to all of the company's employees that they're going to weather the storm and that everyone's jobs was secure, as the company was on a solid foundation. You, the best and most talented people have no worries."

"Wow, that must be a great company," said Slide.

"Not so great," said the King. "The company CEO out-and-out lied to the employees and thirty days later laid off over two-hundred people."

"He lied?"

"Yup, lied through his teeth. He needed the thirty days to get the paperwork done so he could fire everyone. He didn't care about the employees. He only cared about himself and his senior VP's."

"That's a terrible thing to do," said Igor. "What else happened there?"

"They fired people the people that actually did the work, and kept the people who watched the work being done, and then took credit for it," said the King. Slide responded. "So, all of the firings and repositioning were about keeping the VP's and Directors, and eliminating all those that actually had corporate knowledge and talent. Didn't they see that this would hurt them in the long run?"

"Igor, you're so right. In fact, it got very messy as they let some key people go that really were responsible for, let's say, the company's image that had an indirect impact to the bottom line."

Slide interrupted the King. "But your Majesty, that's not making the right decision. That decision is based up moving money to the bottom line so their bonuses kick in."

The King smiled. "I never said that. But that's essentially what happened. When you let go the 'talent' and the people with the 'long term history and knowledge 'or the 'doers' of the company, you create enormously complex situations that will only cost more money in the end."

"How so?" asked Igor.

"When the work can't get done, say for example, the creation of collateral material, they ended up farming it out to an agency at three times the price, three times the turnaround time and three times worse in quality. It was a fiasco, all because the CEO and his reports, who were in it to save their jobs, made the wrong decision."

"So, what do you do?" stated Slide who was thankful that he was not the King.

"The answer is why I'm pacing back and forth. To quote Peter Drucker, '*Management is doing things right; leadership is doing the right things.*'"

"And that means....what?" asked Igor.

"I must make sure I make the right decision or do the right thing, and then I must make sure that management down below me makes the right decisions. They must evaluate and make sure that what they do is for the company, and not in any way used to protect themselves. Too many managers are more interested in saving themselves."

"So, I think Igor and I understand now why you are pacing back and forth."
"Yes, I want to make sure I do the right thing for my Kingdom. That's what my business plan is all about."

With that, the King got up and started to pace again back and forth. Slide got up and followed and Igor brought up the rear.

They were working the problem looking to do what was right.

***The big deal with business planning is knowing when you're done.
A business plan is basically a matrix of decisions in the form of goals
and objectives that can change, and that's why it isn't a report.***

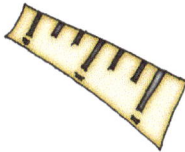

STORY #22
It Is What It Is

"MY FAVORITE SEASON," said the King as he walked with Igor and Slide Rule through the empty Market Square, located in the heart of the Castle.

"What season is that," responded Igor of Moat Designs, Ltd., the all around general contractor for the Castle.

"Hunting season."

"Great, I love a good hunt," said Igor

"Me too," said Slide Rule, from Building Blocks, Inc. who is the Castle's No. 1 architect.

"No. No. You misunderstood me; I'm talking about the Tradeshow Season, where we turn the Market Square into a tradeshow. I'm talking about hunting for new prospects. I'm sure both you and Slide Rule will be having a booth this year."

"Not me," said Igor.

"Me neither, complete waste of time," said Slide agreeing with Igor as he threw up his hand to high five.

"Oh, I'm sure you'll enjoy it. I've made a mandate that all of my Kingdom's main merchants and vendors will both exhibit, and enjoy the experience."

Slide and Igor exchanged glances. "But, I never get any business. It's really a complete waste of time, and the market hours are so long," said Slide.

"Nonsense. Let's sit down and enjoy some fresh cider and I'll share with you the thirteen areas where exhibitors routinely fail in working a tradeshow. If you do these things, you'll get business."

"Thirteen?" said Slide in total disbelief."

"Yes. Thirteen. I'm sure you're going to be excited about each and every one of them." They sat down and cider mysteriously appeared.

"First, your booth should be up-to-date, and have a good location. If it's old looking, then the people passing by will understand that you're an old company and not up-to-date, and that means your ideas are not up to date."

"Second you must have an effective use of technology in the booth. This doesn't mean one flat screen monitor, but interactive case studies showing how your company's solution to a problem will help them."

"Three, there must be a pre-show meeting to motivate the booth workers, and a post-show meeting, to improve the show and get ready for the next one."

"Four, you need to have press release completed and sent out before the show announcing your participation, and you need to make some sort of offer that will generate traffic."

"Five, you must use social media before, during and after the show to keep in touch with the attendees and other prospects, and give them reasons for them to visit your booth."

"Six, the right people must be in the booth."

"Seven, you must not become drunk at parties or even when taking groups of prospects out for dinner."

"Eight, prior to the show, you must concentrate on setting up appointments that will bring prospects and clients to the booth during the show. Other prospects will see this and start to wonder if they should be talking to you. The goal is to get your best clients talking with your prospects."

"Nine, you must have an 'offer' on the show floor that attracts people to the booth."

"Ten, you must follow up on the leads at the end of the show."

"Eleven, you must have a competitive strategy, which means you have a plan to gain competitor information, such as just walking the floor and observe how they conduct themselves, or what their signage says."

"Twelve, you must be one of the seminar speakers. In fact, several people from your office should be speaking. The mere act of public speaking makes you an expert, and that will bring in business."

"Thirteen, don't be something you're not."

Slide and Igor are sitting with a glazed look in their eyes.

"See, that's not so bad," said the King.

Slide poured some more cider. "Your Majesty, with all respect, it's really not possible for me to do all of that."

"For once I agree with Igor," echoed Slide.

"Nonsense. It's just a matter of hiring the right people who understand what it takes to get business. There are experienced people out there who know how to work these shows and make good use of them."

"If I may ask," said Igor, "What does that last one mean – Don't be something you're not. That's confusing to me?"

The King smiled. "That's the most important one about tradeshows, and about business, and life for that matter. If you understand it, your business will profit effortlessly. It is the core of your business plan"

"Tell us more," said Slide excited to hear the explanation.

"Very good. Very good. Now, 'Don't be something your not' means, 'It is what it is.'"

"Well, that clears that up," said Igor.

Igor bursts out laughing.

Slide waved his hand to get attention. "If I understand what you're saying, 'It is what it is' means that prospects and/or employees will eventually find out, so, if you're honest to yourself as a company, particularly at a tradeshow, then you will have overcome a big stumbling block that has certainly slowed the growth of a many companies."

"Yeeaah for Slide," shouted the King.

> *Be honest in your presentation, and in your business deals,*
> *and with your employees, and the news will travel fast,*
> *for people will understand, 'It is what it is.'*
> *Don't be something you're not;*
> *be what you are.*

STORY #23
What's Ahead

THE KING, RULER OF THE LAND, adjusted his seat in the cart being pulled by a team of mules. With him were Igor and Slide and they were on their way to see the King's quarries where the granite blocks were prepared for the large building project the King had commissioned them to build. Slide Rule of Building Blocks, Inc. was the head architect and Igor, from Moat Designs, Ltd. was the general contractor.

Stretched in front of them were the Knights in Shining Armor ready to protect their King from attack. Serfs followed who were ready to serve at the wave of the King's hand.

"What a beautiful day," commented the King to his fellow companions.

Igor made a face. "For you, your Majesty, every day is a beautiful day, for you are King. But for me, today is not a good day."

"And why not?" asked the King.

"I have worries."

"You don't have any worries compared to the worries that I have," commented Slide.

"Could you elaborate, Slide?" asked the King.

"Well, all my problems deal with projects I've had in the past. I even worry about decisions I've made. Were they the right decisions or the wrong decisions? It's an endless string of worries of what might have been, or what might be."

Igor is nodding his head in agreement. "For once I agree with Slide. I have the same problem, but my issues are more than Slide's worries. I worry about everything."

The King 👑 McKenzie

As the countryside slowly passes by, the King pondered the remarks of his chief contractor and architect.

"So," the King said. "It seems this is a problem for you, and I, being your King should help you fix it."

"Oh, don't bother," said Igor with a worried look. "We are quite fine."

Slide took a hint of Igor's anxious words and realized that the last thing they wanted was the King's help. Past lessons had not been pleasant.

"Yes, we are fine. Right with the world, as they say. Please, let's enjoy the countryside on this beautiful day."

The King laughed. "Right you are. We will enjoy the countryside just as soon as I help you."

"Oh gosh," commented Igor giving Slide a dirty look.

The King starts right in. Another Master Class has started. "First, let me tell you that you're both idiots."

Slide buries his face in his hands. Igor puts his hand to his forehead like he had a massive headache.

"First, in life and in business the future is always ahead of you. It's out there waiting for you." The King gestures toward the horizon.

Slide takes a peek and then buries his head again.

"Now, both of you. In the future we will be sitting in a rather small space and it will be enclosed, and we will be looking out a windshield."

"Really?" comments Slide.

"Yes. And in order to see behind you, you will look at a mirror."

Olur.

"What's a mirror," asked Slide.

"A mirror is a shiny surface that reflects what's behind you."

"Like a river on a calm day," said Igor.

"Or, like the blade of a Knights sword?" said Slide smirking at Igor.

"Yes. Very good by the way. But I must ask you a question? Because the windshield is so big, the mirror is very small. What's the reason for that?"

"So you don't block your view," ventured Igor.

"Yes, in a way you're right. But let me put it to you this way. The mirror is small as it represents your past, while the windshield represents your future. You must always look forward and dream about the future and not worry about the past."

"You're so deep," said Slide.

"We have this wonderful day and you're worrying about the past, and you must enjoy the present and look forward to what's ahead of you. This is particularly true in business where one bad experience literally can stay with a company for years. That's the purpose of a business plan, to point your company forward. You must press on. Does that make sense?"

"Yes," said Slide. Igor nodded his head in agreement.

"Have you learned anything Igor?"

"Yes, the past is the past."

In life and in business the future is always ahead of you.

102

STORY #24
Is It Therapy or Consulting?

THE KING SAT AT HIS ROUND TABLE in his designated seat. Behind him were several Knights and a handful of servants ready to serve him at a moments notice. Sitting opposite the all knowing King was Igor owner of Moat Designs, Ltd., and Slide Rule of Building Blocks, Inc. the architect for the Castle.

"So, your Majesty, it is a pleasure to have lunch with you today," said Igor.

"You have lunch with me every Friday at the end of the week," replied the King.

"But today is special," said Slide, "For we have finished a major portion of the work on the East side of the Castle. We'll definitely be finished in just under two years."

"Right on schedule," said Igor.

"Yes, and you both deserve credit for seeing that we meet our goals. But I'm pondering another problem, and it has me a bit overwhelmed at the moment."

"Is it something that Slide and I could help you with, your Majesty?"

"Actually, yes. Maybe both of you. Has anyone here seen a therapist?"

"Nope, not me. I'm completely normal," Slide said with confidence.

"So Slide, you're saying I'm not normal if I saw a therapist?"

"Nooo….Nooo….. I didn't say that" responded Slide who was immediately aware that he was in trouble. Telling the King he was not normal was not a good way to start lunch, or the rest of his life.

"Yes you did. I clearly heard you say that," Igor said.

"For the record, Slide. I'm not going to hold it against you that you said I might not be normal."

"Thank you, your Majesty."

Lunch consisting of hot soup arrived along with some watered down wine. They started to eat and enjoy themselves.

"So, your Majesty, what kind of problem do you have that Slide and I might be able to help you with, if I may be so bold to ask,"

"It's a business issue."

"Then, if it's a business issue shouldn't you be talking to a consultant?"

"Ahaa, a consultant. Yes, I think you're right about that Igor."

"I have read that a consultant, someone, from the outside of your organization who is familiar with the means and methods of your business and industry, can come in and often very quickly identify areas which need improvement, and basically help you lay out a management plan to overcome any challenges and/or to achieve the types of goals that you are after," stated Slide.

"I can't believe you read something," Igor said to Slide.

"You should try it Igor. It would be a new experience for you."

"Okay, cut it out both of you. So tell me, what's the difference between a therapist, and a consultant?"

Slide and Igor sat there with a blank look on their face knowing that they might be getting in too deep. "Don't know," said Slide. Igor shook his head in agreement.

"A therapist spends their time helping someone understand "things" that happened a long time ago, while a consultant deals with existing business conditions and helps determine their future path."

"Wow, you could almost say that a consultant is sort of business therapy," said Igor.

"Very good Igor. But there's even more and it gets even better."

"Here we go…." said Slide to Igor.

The King ignored the remark. "You see, to deal with the past is one way to deal with issues, for it's the past that brings you and what you are to the present. But a consultant's job is to take you into the future. They will ask a series of questions designed to get an idea of who you are, where do you want to go, and then the real work starts, as you will discuss, how do you get there? But they are also accessing the "want" inside of you for they know that it's the "want" and the "attitude" and the "belief" of the leaders that really makes a difference in getting from point A to point B. Much of what a consultant does, through a series of exchanges with the executive staff, is to eventually get everyone to agree on a direction while at the same time getting them to take responsibility for achieving certain benchmarks that are set during the meeting."

"This sounds like a good thing," remarked Slide.

"What do you think, Igor?"

"I trust that having a consultant will certainly be welcomed if they can help with the issues that are on the table."

Perfect." The King turned around and clapped his hands together. A stranger entered with a stack of material and some charts. He sat on the King's right hand side."

The consultant had arrived.

"Is this going to be therapy or consulting," asked Slide.

"Both," responded the wise King. "It's business planning."

Who you are, where do you want to go, and how do you get there?

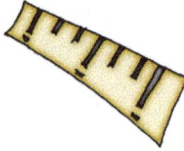

STORY #25
Outside the Box

THE KING ARRIVED AT THE MEETING with Igor, the moat contractor of Moat Designs, Ltd., and Slide Rule the architect of Building Blocks, Inc.

"Sit. I have an idea to contemplate," commanded the King.

Igor and Slide Rule looked at each other knowing they were in for a long one. This usually meant a Master Class. Igor and Slide Rule took their seats on a solid square stone block.

The King continued to pontificate, and pointed to the block. "Do you know what you're sitting on?"

Igor and Slide Rule get up and look at the block. "It's a solid stone block," ventures Igor.

Slide Rule not to be outdone, says, "It's perfectly proportioned three dimensional square stone block."

"Think of it as a box. It's for thinking outside the box," the King says in a stately manner.

"We ARE outside the block, or the box," says Igor.

"Sit down you idiots. It's a business expression meaning to think creatively from a new perspective without any preconceptions. It's usually used as a problem solving tool."

"Good idea. Are we going to think creatively?" asked Igor.

"Can't," said the King.

"Why not?"

"For the same reason why most companies fail. You can't think outside the box until you know what's inside the box."

Igor gets up and looks at the block and scratches his head.

Slide Rule becomes inspired. "That in itself is a very creative statement. Are you sure you're not thinking creatively outside the block right now?"

"I'm sure we're not."

"Tell us more. Let us understand what you understand," said Igor as he sat back down. He smiles at Slide Rule proud of his profound statement. The King walks up and glares at him. Igor shrinks.

"Most companies, and particularly the trades that you two pursue, architecture and construction, have not put into place the infrastructure that is the basis of their business."

"What's an infrastructure?"

"Infrastructure is a framework for business managers to make decisions."

"Such as?"

"A strategic, business and marketing plan."

"That's what's inside the box," asked Igor.

"Yes, you need these tools in place and you need managers that really know how facilitate their use. You need to separate out the real issues of a company and to dissolve them into goals and objectives and to assign responsibilities, and to make people volunteer to be accountable for making the plans work. Then and only then can you start thinking outside the box."

Igor listened carefully. "So, if I may venture an opinion, are you saying that thinking outside the box means that you are looking at different and creative ways to solve the same problems that the infrastructure is addressing inside the box?"

The King broke into a smile. "Right, right, you get it. Sometimes you have to shift your thinking process and look at a situation differently to solve a problem. You said it better then I said it."

Igor smiled. The King smiled. Slide the architect just sat there. Then suddenly Slide had an inspiration.

"If I may," said Slide; "A question. Wouldn't having knowledge of what's inside the box give you preconceived ideas?"

"No. Think of that knowledge or that infrastructure as the benchmark and the springboard for new ideas to occur. To go outside the box, you have to know what's inside the box, so you can develop something that is truly unique and original."

"If I may," said Slide getting up. "How many times has someone thought outside the box and that lead to a disastrous attempt at a solution because they had not addressed the inside the box."

"Hooray," said the King. "You also get it. What a team."

You must use management tools, such as business and marketing plans to manage the people in your business by setting goals and objectives. But you must also think outside the box – which is strategy: what's going to give you a competitive advantage, or what value add is going to get new prospects to knock on your door?

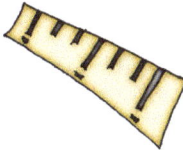

The King 👑 McKenzie

STORY #26
Doing It Well

"GUESS WHAT HAPPENED?" said the King.

The King sat down under a crudely made awning that served to block the harsh summer sun on the edge of the Market Square. Slide Rule of Building Blocks, Inc, the King's No. 1 architect, and Igor, the contractor for the Castle and owner of Moat Designs, Ltd. had already taken a seat. Slide was enjoying his late morning brew.

"Good morning," said Slide.

"Good morning Slide and Igor. I just had an interesting experience." Answered the King.

Igor waved a cheerful hello. "So, tell us what happened?"

"I went into the small shop and the Inn Keeper knew exactly what I wanted. The service was great."

"But you're the King," reminded Slide. "They aren't going to forget your order."

"Well, let's test them. Igor, you've been here before. Go in and see if they remember your order from the last time. If they ask, just say 'the usual' and see what they do."

Igor got up and headed for the door. About ten minutes passed and he came out smiling. "Guess what? They remembered my order. The Barista asked me, 'Do you want your usual; a Verde triple lentil, extra hot, extra shot, double cup with whipped sour goat's milk?' I can't believe he remembered that."

"Now, that's service," commented the King. "There's a lesson there someplace."

"It gets even better. I acknowledged that I was so impressed he remembered my brew. Guess what he said?"

"What?" said Slide and the King in unison?

"He said, 'If you're going to do a job, you might as well do it well.' I'm so impressed."

The King was really pleased. "Wow. That's one dedicated individual. The problem is more people should have those attitudes. Just think what it would be like if everyone behaved that way. Everyone's too busy cutting corners, coming in late, leaving early, over pricing, etc. It's really a terrible problem in society in general."

"It's not our problem. Right Igor," said Slide.

"Yup," answered Igor.

"What do you mean by 'Yup?'" asked the King.

Uh, oh, Igor thought. Here we go. "I meant to say yes."

"That's what I thought you said."

"Is that the right answer," asked Igor.

"No, that's the wrong answer," the King responded. "It's everyone's problem. Let me ask you a question. Have you ever cut corners on a construction project?"

"No," answered Igor with as much authority as he could muster.

"No? Let me as the question again. Have you ever cut corners on a construction project?"

"Ahaaaaa, yes."

Slide hit Igor in the arm. "Are you the village idiot?" exclaimed Slide. "You just told the King, the all knowing King, I might add, that you cut corners. You do most of your work for him. Are you nuts?"

Igor realized his mistake. "Your Majesty let me explain."

"You cheated me?" asked the King.

Igor was trying to visualize what he would look like after spending twenty years in the dungeon. "Not exactly. I took a short cut that saved me money and you ended up with a project you expected."

"Could have I ended up with a better project?"

"Yes. And I feel terrible about it. I mean, look at the guy that served us our coffees. He's doing the job well because that's his job, and I, your trusted contractor, cut corners. I should be fired."

"I agree," said the King.

"Are . . . are you firing me?" asked Igor in a nervous voice.

"No, or course not. You should be fired but I think you can be saved."

"What do I need to do, your Majesty, to be saved?"

"You must agree that if you're going to do a job, that you'll do it well, and that you'll always strive to provide even more service for the money. That's what business planning and strategy is all about. Look for ways to add more value for your clients."

"I can do that," said Igor.

"So can I," responded Slide.

"And I, your all knowing King, will also agree to do that."

The King McKenzie

"What can you do to better your service," asked Igor.

"Just take a fresh breath of air, and think about it," said the King. Then he laughed with great gusto.

Motivate people to do their job well. Are you an example?

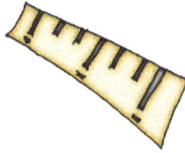

STORY #27
Rules of War

"THE HIGH GROUND IS ALWAYS THE BEST PLACE TO BE when observing war," said the King to Slide Rule and Igor. They had moved to this location to observe the unfolding battle with a neighboring Castle.

"Safety first," said Igor of Moat Designs, Ltd." He and Slide Rule of Building Blocks, Inc. had joined the King to observe the engagement of the King's best troops.

The King sat proudly on his stallion ready for the battle to begin. The timetable was in the trusted hands of his most fearless and accomplished Knights in Shining Armor. "There are many things to be learned from battle, including lessons about business."

"How is that," inquired Slide who was happy up here on the hill as opposed to being down on the battlefield.

"Do you feel safe up here?" inquired the King.

"Yes, most certainly, I do."

"Consider the following statement by Sun Tzu: *'If the enemy is in range, so are you.'*"

"Uh Oh. How does that apply to business?" asked Slide.

"Well, think of it this way. I'm sure that you in your career as an architect you've ventured into new markets and new territories in an effort to increase revenue. By doing so, you also expose your practice to the new competitive forces within that territory. You have to be careful, because if you can compete with them, they can compete with you."

"I never thought of that. You are a wise King."

The King was on a roll. "How about this one? `A sucking chest wound is message for you to slow down.'"

"That's terrible," Igor said. "Is your life one big video game?"

"Yes, but I'll ignore that remark. It's an interesting statement as it's saying in business you need to have balance. Balance between work and play; between home and office. If you don't get balance you end up, metaphorically speaking, with a sucking chest wound."

"Yes, you're right again."

"Business is war, and winning at war is based upon intelligence," said the King.

Slide was getting interested in the conversation. "Well, that sounds meaningful and I can see that it might relate to business. But you know what they say, 'I've got a business to run, I don't have time for all of that stuff.'"

"Ahaa, but Slide, that's where you're wrong. In war, information or intelligence is the critical component to winning because you have the advantage of an informed choice. In fact, in war, intelligence gathering is a full time business. They must know what the enemy is doing or planning to do, so they can react. It's the same for business."

"But it takes time. It's another thing I have to do? I don't have the time for that," complained Igor.

"While you say you have no time for that sort of thing, I say you had better make time, or you'll not have a business. For example, did you know that another contractor moved into the Castle yesterday and is asking around for work?"

"What!" exclaimed Igor. "Another contractor? I didn't know that. This could change everything. Who are they? What kind of work do they do?"

"So what do you think about intelligence gathering now," asked the King.

The King 🪑 McKenzie

"I have taken your point to heart. You're so right. Intelligence gathering is critical."

"How do we go about that?" asked Slide.

"It's not something that you have to add to your list. It's something that becomes part of what you do. Intelligence gathering is part of the business planning process. You listen to what other people say; you essentially become a sponge of information."

"A sponge of information. You have a way with words. But what about this battle in front of us?" asked Slide Rule.

The calmingly King reflected on the battle that would soon start, and then spoke. "In a few minutes I'll give the command to advance. Once I do that we'll move slowly, at first, so they can see the mass of our military slowly moving toward them."

"Will you follow?"

"*'I have to follow them. I am their leader.'* Most likely another Sun Tzu quote. What do you think, Slide?"

"I think you're at your quota."

The King looks at Slide. "You should be in the military."

"Why?"

"Because you are very, very brave."

If you can't see your competitors around you, it doesn't mean they're not there.

Note: "If the enemy is in range, so are you," is by Sun Tzu. It was also a favorite quote by General MacArthur. "I have to follow them. I am their leader," is also most likely a quote by Sun Tzu.

116

STORY #28
Not Inside; Outside

THE KING WALKED INTO THE DESIGN STUDIO of Slide Rule of Building Blocks, Inc., the head architect for the Castle. Slide was having breakfast with Igor from Moat Designs, Ltd., who was the general contractor for the Castle, was sitting next to him.

"It's nice to see you caught up on your work," said the King. A three-legged stool was immediately provided for the King by a Serf that always traveled with the King.

"What a wonderful surprise. May I offer you and your Serf breakfast? We're having biscuits and gravy with sausage, bacon and ham on the side. We have plenty."

"That actually sounds good. Thank you."

The King's Serf takes a seat at the table, and Igor gets up and serves them both.

The King starts to eat his breakfast. "Why aren't the two of you out on job sites?"

"Well, we do have some pending work to do on the Castle, but we're waiting for the granite blocks to arrive from the quarry," said Igor.

"Usually when you don't have work to do here, you're both busy doing other projects. What's going on?"

Slide thought for a second, and then responded. "We're waiting for work to come in the front door."

"I have to admit one thing – you do sound just like an architect."

"Why do you say that your Majesty" said Igor.

The King 🪑 McKenzie

"A famous architect-consultant by the name of Ron McKenzie *(shameless self–promotion)*, wrote in a book a long time ago, that said the way architect's market is they sit in their office and wait for the phone to ring."

"Phone?"

"A future thing. Don't worry about it. I don't think you would use it. However, let me ask you a question. If you want more work, where is it?"

Slide and Igor looked at each other. They realized another Master Class was now is session.

Slide took the bait. "Your Majesty, the work is located outside the office."

"Very well put Slide," replied the King.

A sheepish smile broke out on Slide's face; he looked at Igor to flaunt his pride of getting the answer right. He went back to his biscuits and gravy.

"Now. I have another question. Igor, why don't you answer this one. If the work is located outside of the office, why are you sitting inside the office?" Igor looked at Slide knowing it was a trap.

"Your Majesty, the reason that Slide and I are sitting here, at Slide's invitation by the way, is we feel the best way to get work is to be ready for it when it walks in the door,"

"Good answer," said the King.

Igor looked very proud.

"But the absolutely wrong answer. You're both idiots."

Slide and Igor slumped down on their three legged stools, putting down their spoons. The Serf moved to another table.

"It's a lot of work to go out and talk to people," reasoned Slide.

118

"So, are you saying you have a free ride here?"

"Oh, no. no, no . . . ." said Igor in total fear.

"What's interesting, is, it seems sometimes when firms get to a certain level, unless they're managed by people with real business sense, the tendency is to let their architectural work speak for them. Design a beautiful building and the work will just slide into the office without any effort. No pun intended, Slide."

"Are you saying that even firms that have several principals have the same problem?"

"Yes. It's actually worse for them because they don't even know they have a problem."

"So, what should we do?"

"It's real easy. If you don't have work, get out of the office. Start with past clients. They're the easiest to get business from. Then move on to your prospect list. Next, look at the associations that your prospects belong to, and join them and start attending meetings and joining committees. Make some speeches. You must market, market and market. Step out of your comfort zone and go to work."

"You know, I just realized something, you're so right. I'm so far behind in my marketing, I could spend the next month visiting my past projects and clients."

"Your right," said Igor.

"You see, even though we're talking about marketing, we're really talking about business planning."

"Really," said Slide.

"Yes, the business plan sets the direction for the marketing plan. And by the

119

way, you're both going to spend at least the next month doing exactly that. Maybe longer."

"How's that going to happen, your Majesty?"

The King turned around and hailed a Knight in Shining Armor. "Sir Knight. Please notify the quarry to delay the shipment of stone blocks."

"Very well, you're Majesty." The Knight respectfully bowed, and turned to leave. Another Knight took his place.

The King turned back toward Slide and Igor. They were no where to be seen. They were both out of the office.

Marketing and sales is a never ending task. Owners and principals must make speeches, write articles in magazines, attending association meetings; you want them to see that you're interested in what they do. Delegation is a way to multiply your marketing presence; it's not an excuse to hide in an office.

STORY #29
What's On Your Plate?

SLIDE RULE SLUMPED DOWN ON TO A STOOL. The owner of Building Blocks, Inc., the No. 1 architect working on the Castle was very tired.

"You look beat," said the jubilant King.

The very dejected Slide looked up at the happy King. "It's easy for you to be happy. You're the King and everything is done for you. As for me, I have to do everything myself, and I have all these problems and things I need to get done. I get overwhelmed to the point I can't move."

"Just ignore everything," stated Igor, owner of Moat Designs, Ltd., a general contractor. "That's what I do."

"Igor, that's why you're in such of a financial mess," said the King.

"Thanks for reminding me."

The King started to pace. This was not a good sign.

"Why don't the two of you pull up some chairs and listen to my wisdom. My Master Class is now in session."

"I can't do that," said Slide. "I've got too much to do and not enough time to do it."

"Right," said Igor. "I agree with Slide. You, the King, have nothing to worry about. And besides, as Slide pointed out, everything is done for you."

"Really, is that what you think?"

Igor and Slide exchange glances, and then both nod their head in agreement.

"Okay," the King said thoughtfully. "I'll tell you what, I'm going to brief you what's on my plate, and how I manage it. This is valuable for everyone, but particularly those in construction industry as there are so many details you are responsible for, or a project could go bad very quickly. However, you must promise not to tell anyone, as these are my secrets. These are very confidential and are known as the King's Secrets. If you told anyone, the consequences would be dire. Am I clear on this point?"

"We understand," replied Slide for both he and Igor.

"Okay. First of all, the neighboring King has sent a message to me that if we don't abandon the corn and wheat fields to the north, he's going to attack our Castle and tear it down to the ground. Also, I got word through another messenger that there's been an outbreak of an unknown disease to the west of us, and it seems to be traveling in this direction. It's literally killing people right and left. Last night the horses got out from the stable, and these were some of the best trained war horses we have. If we don't get them back, we're going to be very vulnerable to an attack. On top of that, there hasn't been a good storm for quite some time, and if we don't get any rain, it could be considered a drought, and that will impact our winter food supply. Also, to the west someone has made camp and has been watching my Castle. We think it's another King from another area that has their eyes on this piece of land, because the farm land fertile and drains well. I also got word from my Senior Knight that we might have an in-house spy. They are deeply buried and we don't have a clue who it is or who they are spying for. Oh, and one more thing, one of my Knights heard that several Serfs are unhappy, and are gearing up for an internal revolt. If I don't address that, and everything else, I'm going to be in big trouble. There's more, but I won't burden you with the details."

Slide and Igor looked at the King in silence with eyes like owls. They both realized that they had nothing on their plate compared to the burden the King was carrying.

"How do you remain so happy and in control?" asked Slide "You're always conveying to us a very confident outlook on life. How can you do that with those kinds of burdens, which in fact, will impact all of us, and even change

122

our lives?"

"The answer is very simple, and you can use the same technique that I do to manage all of the stuff of life."

"But your stuff of life is really a lot more than the things we carry around with us. I had no idea."

"So, what's the secret," asked Igor.

"The secret is in a book authored by James Clavell, titled Noble House. It's about big business in Hong Kong in the sixties, and focuses on seven days in the life of the tai-pan, Ian Dunross, the leader if the *Noble House*. When asked how he manages his burdens Dunross explained *'. . .that the only way to deal with problems was the Asian way: to put them into individual compartments and take them up only when ready for them.' He went on to say that 'If you can't you'll go under – ulcers, heart attack, old before your time, your health broken.'"*

Slide and Igor sat there in silence.

The King continued. "What Clavell was saying through his character Ian Dunross was that you must free up your mind of your everyday burdens. Literally, visualize yourself putting them in a box, and locking them up. When you need to address them, take them down and do what you have to do. You get what you think about, so don't think about the bad stuff."

"So you're saying, if you carry them around with you, you become like Slide. He's so overwhelmed he doesn't know which one to do first. Don't let your problems get in the way of living."

"Very good Igor. Yes, that's exactly what I'm saying."

Slide was impressed. "You're a good King. Now I'm worried about all of the other things that are happening in the Kingdom. What else do you have that helps you?"

"Joss."

Don't let the stuff of the world overwhelm you. Manage them one-by-one, prioritize, and seek solutions that minimize risk.

Also, "Joss" is a Chinese colloquial expression that came to be known as "luck".

STORY #30
What Contract?

"SO, IGOR, WHAT'S THE PROBLEM? It's the end of the day, and you're usually happy when we get together for a brew," said the King to his No. 1 contractor and owner of Moat Designs.

Sitting with them was Slide Rule, the King's No. 1 architect who took a sip of his watered down wine. "Is it the new project you're doing?"

The three of them had sat down on three legged stools in the shade outside a pub and eatery. The King's servants hovered nearby ready to assist the King.

Slide turns toward the King. "He's got a little project outside the Castle walls."

"Thanks for that Slide," responded Igor.

"Igor, are you doing work for others?" asked the King.

Igor looked at the King, knowing he might now be in trouble. "I'm sorry your Majesty. I just wanted to pick up some extra shillings."

"Igor, my friend, it's fine with me that you're getting extra work. Good for you." Igor looked relived.

"So, what's the situation? Tell us about it, perhaps Slide and I can help."

"Well, the project started out fine, but now that it's done, the owner is upset. He said I didn't do what he asked."

The King waved for another round of drinks. "Sounds like that's simple to correct. Just show him the paperwork as to what you've agreed to do, and that should settle it. You know, contract, plans and specifications, project reports, material delivery, change orders, progress photos, closeout documents, punch list . . . the usual."

Igor was silent. Slide was silent. The King was silent. Then, the King became angry.

"Are you saying to me in your silent way of communicating that you have no paperwork?"

"Yes, I have no paperwork."

"You're an idiot."

"I agree," said Slide.

"Do you know what the famed Hollywood movie producer Robert Evans once said?" asked the King.

"Movie producer?" responded Igor.

"It's a future thing. Don't worry about it. So Igor, do you know what Robert Evans said?"

"No your Majesty."

"How about you Slide?"

"No, I'm not even sure I know what the word movie means."

The King took a sip of his wine, and for dramatic effect, stood up to address them both. Another Master Class had started.

"Robert Evans said the following . . ."
"There are three sides to every story:
Your side, my side, and the truth.
And no one is lying.
Memories shared serve each differently."

126

"That really clears everything up," said Igor sarcastically.

The King just stares at Igor.

"Sorry your Majesty. Could you explain that to me?"

"In your case, it concerns the delivery of professional services, but it also applies to those that manufacture a product, provides a service, and even to the retail market that sells the product. There must be clear documentation as to what is being delivered, no matter who you are."

"Waste of time," said Slide.

"Really?" said the King. "Are you saying that providing me with a contract is a waste of time?"

"No, no your Majesty. It's just time consuming. I just don't see how it can help."

"Well, look at your buddy Igor. He's probably going to get involved in a long court case that will take time and money. Lots of money."

"So, proper documentation can save you money?"

"Yes. That's exactly what I'm saying. You see, going back to the quotation by Robert Evans. Igor has 'his' side of the story. His client has 'their' side of the story. And then there's always the truth, or what really happened. Memories tend to fade. People exaggerate to try and win."

Igor's mood brightened. "If I understand correctly, documentation helps get to the truth. If I had to go to court I could just present the documents to the Judge and tell them, this is our agreement, this is what I charged, this is what I delivered. I did it on-time and under-budget. There were no safety violations and the punch list is done. Is that what you're saying?"

"Yes. You got it," responded the happy King.

"But what are they going to do now? I mean, they're fighting," asked Slide.

"The only thing he can do is to apply reason. Get all of your notes together and sit down with them and lay out what you felt was the agreement and try and talk to them. If there's a difference, then make an offer to correct it, and if it's new work that you would have had to charge them for, then . . . can you tell me the answer Igor?"

"Get it in writing."

"Splendid."

Do you have a paper trail? Do you have records of what happened and when? Remember, the documentation of a project, from start to finish is a PROCESS – nothing more.

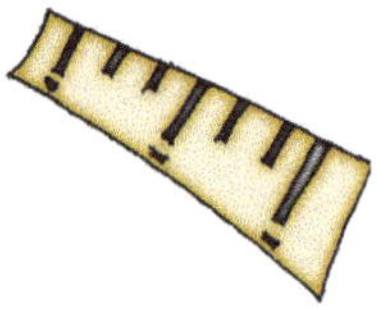

The King ♔ McKenzie

STORY #31
In Search of Leadership

THE KING WAS IN TOP SINGING FORM. "All together now, one, two, three, keep your mind on your driving, keep your hands on the wheel, keep your snoopy eyes on the road ahead. . . "

"Your Majesty, I have a problem," said Slide Rule, the No. 1 architect of the Castle, interrupting the King's presentation.

The King was at the front of the small group of Knights and business owners that worked the marketplace to sell their wares. The King had been leading them in a management exercise. "What is that, Slide," asked the King.

Everyone stood as if they were a frozen statue, as someone had dared to address the King. "Well, said Slide, "I was talking with Igor and he said he doesn't understand what you're talking about."

"Hey, don't bring me into this," said Igor, the King's No. 1 contractor.

"Okay. Let's take a break." The King slapped his hands together almost expecting the lights to go out.

Everyone sort of disbanded and they went to sit in the shade. Watered down wine was immediately served the King. He glanced at the group, and waved his hand. Magically, wine was served to everyone.

"What part don't you get?" asked the King.

"I don't get any of it," answered Igor. "I have no idea what's going on."

"So the situation is status quo," said Slide in a mocking voice.

Everyone in the room turned and looked at Slide in fear, including the King. There were no sounds to be heard.

129

"That's a good one," said the King in a laughing voice." Everyone breathed a sigh of relief.

"What we've been talking about is leadership. A business person must have leadership in their company just like a Knight needs to have leadership on the battlefield."

"Your Majesty, tell us more about leadership."

"It's my pleasure. First of all, what I'm worried about is the lack of leadership in today's modern society. The gossip and rumor mills are filled with many stories where managers are letting down their employees, even small companies of around twenty-five people. It's unbelievable that so many managers don't have a clue what leadership means."

The King continued. "There are three main considerations concerning leadership: What is it, where did it go, and how do we get it back?"

Igor raised his hand out of politeness. "I'll get things started. "What is leadership?"

"Very good Igor. Leadership is the ability to manage the big picture, such as future market positioning, all the way down to the smallest detail. It's the ability to relate to their largest customers, as well as to the janitor that sweeps the floor. It's the ability to set in place processes that provide a structure for multiple employees to do their job. Quite frankly, leadership is all about respect in all areas of the business. It's also about reacting to new threats. It's lacking in many companies."

"Respect?" said Slide.

"Yes, respect. So often the leaders of a company cannot identify with the challenges of their employees, both on a business and a personal level. Being a leader and demonstrating leadership means you understand and have empathy and you, the leader, are there to help them. Saying things like, 'this is not working' to someone means that you have failed to lead. Leadership is about people."

"Wow," said Slide. "I had no idea that leadership was about people. But, where did it go?"

"Leadership has given way to the financial report. It's often said there are two ways to manage a company. One way is from a marketing aspect, which is more closely aligned with people. The second way is from a financial over-view. While financials are absolutely necessary in making decisions, it's not a substitute for taking people out of the equation. True leaders lead people, not numbers. The numbers are simply a scorecard. Leadership is absent in most companies and the scorecard is in its place."

The King continued. "In good times companies are led from a marketing perspective, in bad times they're lead from a financial statement. The real dirty little secret of business is that it always should be lead from a market-ing perspective. That's what a leader does."

"So, how do we get it back?" asked Igor.

"You must fight for it. You must be a Knight in Shining Armor. You must man-age from the bottom."

Slide raised his hand. "Your Majesty, what does manage from the bottom mean?"

"It means you must always lead even if those above you are a confused tangled web of decision making with no direction or even a concept of lead-ership. You must never become a roadblock when others depend upon you. You must set an example. You must train those around you even though they have no idea you are training them."

"But, what's the point?"

"The point is, you know you have done the right thing. You have leadership with what you have responsibility for, and you try and help those above you trying to point out the right direction and decision. Even if you fail, you have won."

"How is that?" asked Slide.

"It's all about respect for yourself and going home at night knowing that you are doing more than the best job possible. You are a leader of leadership. That's what's meant by "... *keep your mind on your driving, keep your hands on the wheel...*"

Being a leader means you must make decisions based upon what is best for the company now, and in the future. Too often leadership is interpreted as a balance sheet. Real leaders know the financial is the scorecard of marketing. If there's a problem, fix the problem, meaning your services and products you offer, and market them. To cut marketing and advertising means you are cutting the primary resource of the business. The real problem of those that manage from a financial perspective is changing the numbers doesn't solve the problem.

Note: The music lines came from *Seven Little Girls (Sitting In The Back Seat)* by *Paul Evans & The Curls.* Writer(s): Lee Pockriss, Bob Hilliard.

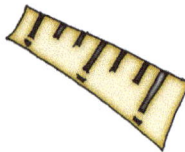

STORY #32
The Inbox

"SO, WHERE'S YOUR PRICE?" asked the King.

"What price?" replied Igor, the No. 1 contractor of the Castle and owner of Moat Designs. Igor, Slide Rule and their King were all taking a walk to view latest construction changes in the Castle and particularly the Moat, which had been leaking.

"The one I asked for."

"I didn't get it."

"I left it in your Inbox," said the King.

"Oh, Oh."

"What does 'Oh, Oh' mean," asked the King.

"It means that... that...that... I'm so, so sorry, your Majesty. I never looked in my Inbox."

"Is that why it's piled so high? I just thought you were busy."

"Igor, that is truly an unacceptable performance," stated Slide Rule, the King's No. 1 architect and owner of Building Blocks, Inc.

The King turns and gives Slide Rule 'the look.' "Who are you to criticize Igor? Your Inbox was higher than his Inbox."

Igor smiles at this news and mocks the King behind his back.

"I wouldn't do that if I were you, Igor," said the King

Igor immediately stops.

"Did you ever even think that my guards standing all around me can actually see and talk?"

Igor suddenly knows that his life is probably in great danger. "I didn't mean anything by it, your Majesty. Please believe me."

"I'll tell you what, how about the three of us have a seat over here in the Fermented Wine Garden and enjoy a glass and we'll talk about the psychological factors involved with people who do not use their Inbox."

They start to move toward the garden. "Sounds good to me responded Igor."

They gather around a small wooden table and water down wine is served to the King who tastes it and waves his approval. "First of all, people who do not use their Inbox properly are suffering from what they refer to as 'Litter-Box Syndrome.'"

"My Siamese cat Mr. Blue has that same problem," Slide said.

"So do you," responded the King. "You probably learned it from your cat Mr. Blue."

"Let me continue. The Inbox was invented as a way to expedite paperwork. The idea is, which apparently the two of you completely missed, is to actually lift the piece of paper out of the Inbox and either, one, take it to your office for review and take immediate action, or two, forward it to someone with a note, or three, discard it in the junk mail immediately."

The King's lecture continues. "The Inbox is not a depository of work 'To Do.' It is not to be used as an excuse for not doing something you should be doing. It's meant to create a seamless flow of information so business within a group can be conducted. It's not a storage bin. It's not a place to put papers that you don't want to lose. It's a Management 101 tool, pure and simple. It's a process."

"Well that makes good sense," said Igor as he thought about it.

The King ♟ McKenzie

"You know, it's going to get worse because someday everyone will have e-mail Inboxes, some people will have multiple Inboxes, and they'll learn to go through them on a regular basis or they will get too far behind. But for you two, this is a disgrace."

"E-mail?"

"It's a future thing. So why don't both of you use it?"

"Well, it's like this; it's a way to differ potential problems. If I don't know about it, how can I be responsible?"

"I ask for a price to give you some work, and you don't respond. What does that say about how much you like working for me, especially in these tough economic times?"

Igor takes sip and makes a grimace at the vinegary taste of the wine. "I see your point, your Majesty," said Igor is a raspy voice.

"Just remember what Peter F. Drucker said."

"Uh, it's on the tip of my tongue," replied Slide.

"Is that sarcasm," asked the King of Slide. "Are you mocking me?"

"No, no. Ahaaa, yes, yes it was. It was meant as a joke."

"Bad joke. Wrong time."

"Yes your Majesty."

"Anyway, Drucker said, '*Efficiency is doing things right; effectiveness is doing the right things.*'"

"Really, Igor said.

"So now what are the two of you going to do after this meeting?"

"Check out our Inbox," they both said in unison.

"Another round," said the smiling King.

You must establish a process for everything in your office.
Developing a process means you are managing by improving
efficiency, and efficient companies make money.

STORY #33
Sweat Equity

THE KING WAS IN A VERY GOOD UPBEAT MOOD. The owner of the Castle walked into the room and was literally glowing. Slide Rule of Building Blocks, Inc, the King's No. 1 architect, and Igor, of Moat Designs, the contractor for the Castle, were slumped at a table finishing a noon day meal consisting of huge slabs of ribs, a pheasant or two, and a lump of cheese all washed down with watered down wine. It was all they could do to stay awake.

"I had a great workout today," said the King.

Slide gave the King a half hearted wave of acknowledgement. It must have been that second pheasant he ate that was making him so sleepy.

"You know, if you exercised a bit more, you wouldn't get so tired."

Slide looked up. "That doesn't make any sense at all."

"But it's true. Have you ever exercised?" inquired the all knowing King.

"Once, but I quit."

"Why?"

"The gym was on the second floor."

"Soooooo….help me understand?"

"I had to walk up a flight of stairs just to exercise."

"Do you ever think before you speak? The purpose of exercise is to exercise.

Man, you really must be out of shape?"

"It's a drag to walk up stairs to exercise."

"I've got an idea for you. How about if a I shared a way to increase produc-tivity of all your employees, make them feel better, and in general, improve their overall health?"

"Sounds good to me," said Igor who had almost fallen asleep. He was always interested in increasing productivity.

"Here's the idea. Everyone who works for you takes off for thirty minutes at some point during the day to walk for about twenty minutes."

"There is no way I'm going to pay anybody to walk while they're working for me," said Igor.

"No, no. You don't get the point. All kinds of magical things happen when a person exercises. This has been proven over-and-over again. Your employees get a mental break. They'll walk with a friend and talk about their family and sports, which they already do on company time. Their heart rate goes up a bit and they get to stretch their muscles. This will help increase greater productivity when they get back to the office."

Igor shook his head. "No."

"No? It has been studied over-and-over again. It will help your business and lower medical cost. It's a win-win situation."

Slide and Igor are very sleepy and barely awake.

The King is now flexing his muscle. "You know what, I think this is a good idea. A really good idea. Let's put a plan-of-action together."

Slide is seeing that the King is getting serious. "I really don't think we need a program like that. Really, it will increase my costs, and I can't afford it right now."

"Nonsense!
"I'm positive that both of your companies will benefit. I think we should get together and work out a detailed plan."

"That's not necessary," said Igor sensing danger approaching.

"I insist. In fact, as the King and Owner of this Castle, and the major employer, I'm hereby requiring that all major vendors such as you, have an in-house company exercise program. In fact, I have a small cabin by the lake, and we can go there as sort of a retreat, and work out the details."

"We couldn't possibly trouble you," said Slide.

"Nonsense. Are you in or are you out?"

"But if I were out, then we might not get work from you."

"Exactly. When you're out, you're out. Are you in or are you out?"

Slide and Igor answer as if they belonged to a chorus. "In."

"Good. Let's get started."

"But that's a long trip. It will take a lot of effort to get the horses and carts set up and ready to go."

"I've got news for you. We're walking."

A company's business plan can address many different issues under the heading of increasing efficiency. If a company helps their employees, they will work harder and be proud of where they work. It's also a wonderful publicity tool.

STORY #34
The Law of the Billiard Table

THE KING WALKED PROUDLY THROUGH HIS MARKET SQUARE with Igor, the moat builder for the Castle, on one side of him, and Slide Rule, the architect for the Castle, on his other side. The King was proud, the sky was blue and everything was good.

"So, Igor and Slide, it's a new year, I assume both of you have your business plans ready."

Slide glances at Igor and makes a face.

"Actually, I'm quite close to finishing it. But I never know if I have enough, and whether I need to add more tactics, or expand the ones I already have," said Igor.

"Very good. How about you Slide?"

"To be honest, I haven't started yet. Last year's plan should be good enough."

"That's what you said last year. How old is your plan? Be honest now."

"At least three years old, your Majesty."

"Typical for most businesses. What if something unexpected happens?"

Slide takes a gamble, and decides to debate the King. "Your Majesty, even though my plan is old, it's good, and if something happens, I'm sure that the plan will provide me guidance and wisdom."

"I understand. Have either one of you ever heard of the Law of the Billiard Table?"

"No," said Slide. "What's a Billiard Table?"

"It's a future thing. I actually have one, but please understand, this is my little secret. I'd like to show you what it is. I think you'll find it interesting."

The King, now surrounded by his Knights, signaled for Igor and Slide to follow. They eventually arrived at a East Corner Tower, and entered the guarded doorway, and started to climb the steps. Round-and-round they went until eventually they arrived at the top. When they entered the chamber, before them was a green felt billiard table."

"What's that," asked Slide?"

"It's a billiard table, also referred to as a pocket pool table. Sometimes I come up here in the evenings and play. Let me demonstrate the game."

Cold brew was immediately served, and as Slide and Igor watched, the King took down a pool cue from the wall, and started to demonstrate the finer points of the game. After a while, there were only two balls left on the table. The white ball, known as the cue ball, was sitting down at one end of the table, and the red ball was at the other end partly overhanging the corner pocket.

"Now," said the King. "The white ball is sitting at this end of the table, and it represents your strategic, business and marketing plan. The implementation of the plan is when you strike the cue ball and it rolls down the table and hits the red ball. When the red ball drops into the pocket, it represents that your plan is successful, meaning all your goals and objectives are met, and you are profitable."

"Wow," said Igor. "That's a great way to look at it."

"Okay, now, I'm going to move the white cue ball all the way down the table and place it about a foot away from the overhanging red ball and also at an angle. It's an easy shot because almost half of the red ball is overhanging the pocket. And because of the angle, there's no way the white cue ball can end up in the pocket. Same situation, but closer. There is no chance that you can miss, meaning in our analogy, that there's no way your strategic, business and marketing plan is not going to be profitable. Right?"

"Right," they both said.

"Wrong."

"What!"

"You're both wrong."

"Please explain," said Igor.

"The Law of the Billiard Table states there is no possible way for you to miss the shot, meaning of course in our analogy, that your business plans will be successful. However, what I'm telling you is there is always something that you don't know."

"How so?"

"What if a meteorite is headed toward earth and strikes the pool table just as you take the shot? The result is, the shot is missed. The Law of the Billiard table says you should have made the shot. But remember, there's always something you don't know, and that's the reason for business planning. You must have contingency plans as part of your business plan."

"So, that means we don't know what we don't know, and the business plan, if done correctly, helps us prepare for the unknown. It would follow then that all business plans must be updated on a regular basis."

"Slide! Your got it. Good for you!"

Igor raises his hand. "So what you're also saying, is that the closer the cue ball is to the red ball, meaning you have a very detailed plan with a lot of "what if's" addressed, the better chance you have in making the plan, but it still means you must always manage the plan, as there are always unknowns lurking about."

"Yeaaaaa, for Igor."

There are many unknowns in business, and all of the business planning tools, such as a strategic, business and marketing plans, plus special plans, such as acquisition plans, can help you prepare for that meteorite hurdling through space.

The Law of the Billiard Table was first mentioned in Ian Flemings' novel *From Russia, With Love* first published in 1957. For more information on The Law of The Billiard Table, go to my Compass Consulting Web site: http://www.compassconsultantscorp.com/Billiards.html

STORY #35
Learning to Love Marketing

"CUT!" YELLED THE KING.

Slide Rule, chief architect of Building Blocks Inc., immediately stopped what he was doing. "Maybe you should get another actor," pleaded Slide.

"That's a great idea," suggested Igor trying to rescue Slide from the madness of the King.

"Nonsense, Igor. Instead, why don't you join Slide in our little movie?"

Igor, of Moat Designs, Ltd., a construction company specializing in moats, reluctantly joined Slide.

"The King surveyed his troupe of players. "Ready, set . . . ACTION."

They proceeded to very badly act out their roles, until they heard the rather uptight voice of their King.

"CUT," screamed the King.

"That's what I just did with my marketing department," said Igor.

Slide laughed at this historically.

The King, calls for a break, and they all moved to the shade of a gigantic oak tree. Refreshments were immediately served.

"Now, Igor. Tell me, why did you cut marketing? You can't be serious? This is a recession; you can't stop marketing. It's against the law," exclaimed the King.

Slide Rule looked for a chance to defend his friend. "Your Majesty. If I may point out, there's no law that says you can't cut marketing."

"It's my Kingdom. I make the laws. Therefore, I bequeath that you cannot cut marketing. It is done."

"I have to cut expenses someplace," responded Igor weakly.

"So you cut the lifeblood of future business? Does that make any sense, Igor?"

"Yes."

"Why does it make sense?" asked the King.

"I don't know why it makes sense?"

"Wouldn't it be better to expand marketing? To invest in that one area of business that can bring in work by developing new market approaches or by developing a spin on your brand, or by showing people how they can actually put money in their pocket by using your services."

"But your Majesty," responded Slide. "In defense of Igor, no one expands marketing in a down market. The general rule of thumb is to cut expenses to save money for the future economic boom that we're all waiting for."

"So, Slide, let's assume for a fraction of a second divided by one-thousand, that you're right. Let me ask this question; If everyone is cutting back on marketing, wouldn't that mean your marketing shillings would go further – that you would get more out of it. Your company would get more attention that you could make an impression on someone using your services. That could change your business?"

"Yes, but ...."

"So, if you can get more bang for your shilling, as they say, what are you waiting for?" asked the King.

Slide looked lost and then launched in with full confidence. "I'm waiting for the retrograde to get over with before I launch any new programs?"

145

Igor laughed out loud and the King shot him a look.

The King brightened with a smile. "Astrology. Actually, that's a very good and wise answer if we were in a retrograde, but we're not, so you're going to have to do better than that."

Igor thought for a moment. "Well, it's because that's what we've been taught – that marketing is expendable."

"Who taught you?"

"Our Chief Financial Officer," responded Slide.

"Maybe he's misleading you so he's not cut?"

"Oh. I never thought of that."

"It's called job security."

"But, If I cut advertising, direct mail and other marketing programs, that money is moved right over to the bottom line. Now I have a chance at making my yearly goals. And besides, no one is buying so why waste the money. That's what I've been taught."

"Very good Slide. You answered as you have been taught. So I'm here to re-teach you – to put you on a path of profitability."

"Okay, I'm all ears."

'So am I," said Igor.

"Okay," said the King in his best marketing voice. "Here's what you need to know. First, in a recession or bad times, you must always reinvent yourself so you are attracted to the market. In business plans it's referred to as positioning. This is a critical and achievable step. Second, don't fall into the trap that marketing is expendable. In actuality, the marketing and business developers working for you are the ones that are absolutely the most valuable to your company."

"Wow. That's pretty good advice," said Igor.

"Yes, to survive in a recession you must first learn to love your marketing department, and if you must, you cut other expenses. But you must, must . . . must, expand marketing your marketing."

"Marketing your marketing. I like that," said Slide.

> *Don't fall into the scenario where the financial people run the company. The only thing they see are numbers; they are scorekeepers, not the coach. You must make decisions based upon a marketing mindset backed up with marketing tactics.*

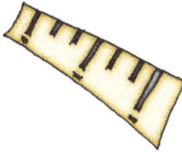

STORY #36
Suspects, Prospects, Clients and Allies

THE KING, SLIDE RULE, AND IGOR were out for their daily constitutional. Following closely behind them were the Knights in Shining Armor who always accompanied their King.

"So, Igor, you're my most dependable moat contractor. If I may ask, what do you attribute your success too?"

Igor, owner of Moat Designs, was quite animated in his response. "Well, your Majesty, while I'm successful, sometimes I think I should be a lot more successful."

"Slide, you're the owner of Building Blocks, Inc., what do you think?"

"To be honest, I agree with Igor. We are each successful in our own way. But we could do better in obtaining more clients."

They arrived at a shady spot overlooking the river near the Castle. "Let's stop here for a rest and a bite to eat."

Immediately everything they needed appeared before them.

"This might be a good time for another Master Class," announced the King.

A cold brew was offered to them as Igor rolled his eyes at the thought of another Master Class.

The King who had his back to Igor said," I wouldn't act that way if I were you, Igor."

Igor was shocked that he had been caught mocking the King. "Oh my, I'm so sorry."

"No problem. Both of you just listen to what I have to say. You both need

148

more work, right?"

"Yes," they both answered in unison.

"If that's the case, consider this quote – '*I am a part of all that I have met.*'"

Igor and Slide just looked at each other. Slide decided to speak out. "Your Majesty, those are very profound words, but they mean nothing to us."

"I could have guessed that. That was a quote from *Ulysses* by Alfred Lord Tennyson. He was saying that everyone you meet has an influence on who you are today."

"Makes no sense to me at all," said Igor.

"I suspected that. So listen and I'll give you an example. But first, how many contacts do you have in your suspects, prospects, clients and allies database?"

Igor and Slide exchange worried glances. "Database?" questioned Slide.

"It's a future thing. Do you have any contacts at all?"

"I have a client list, but I don't correspond with them as I've already done their work," answered Slide.

"Listen, you must always market to your clients for two reasons; one, they will come back to you for more work, and two, they can also refer someone to use your services. They also become one of your allies. You must of course market to suspects, someone who might use your services, but needs a push to move into the next category, and that is a prospect. You must market to a prospect until they sign your contract. The last categories are allies."

"Are you saying there are other people who are allies besides your clients?" said Igor.

"Yes. An ally is someone who is a chief recommender to your company, someone who can make a difference by making a phone call, sending an email, or just telling someone, that if you're going to do a project you need to have Slide do it."

"Okay. Who are these allies?"

"They come from your professional network, such as architects, engineers, lawyers, sub-contractors and people you know in your social network. Consider this story – a business developer who was also responsible for marketing, had an outstanding reputation with a wide professional network. He was let go from the company he was working for, so he went into consulting. The business developer could have become a great ally to his former company as he had the network, knew the players, projects and the market. But instead they never bothered to contact him in any way."

"Wow. I can even see the benefit of making him a friend of the company. That was a big mistake. Huge," said Igor.

Slide was getting excited. "So, what you're saying is we really need to concentrate on marketing in those four different categories?"

"Exactly right," answered the King.

"But I have a question. How does this tie into the quotation by Alfred Lord Tennyson – *'I am a part of all that I have met.'*"

"Think about it. It means that everyone you meet in your life and in your business, shape you. Your environment shapes you, and you become the person who you are because of the people you meet and the experiences you have, including suspects, prospects, allies and clients."

"I got it," said Igor. "It's why we hang around you, the King. We become part of you and because of that, we are a better person."

"Hooray for Igor!"

Because of database marketing techniques and contact manager software programs, it's relatively easy for a marketing coordinator to manage a database of suspects, prospects, allies and clients. Each group is marketed to differently based upon your company's marketing strategy and tactics. This database development can become a very valuable asset of the company; in fact, it's not uncommon for a company to acquire another company because of their database.

STORY #37
The Ox and the Horse

IGOR SAT ON AN OX. The King's No. 1 contractor and owner of Moat Designs, was thoroughly disgusted.

The King of the Castle, and Slide Rule, owner of Building Blocks, Inc. stood looking up at Igor.

"As the King's architect, I wish you speedy travels and a good and safe trip," said Slide. He then laughed hysterically.

The King, being the King, was serious in his demeanor. Then he too broke out in a fit of laughter. "Igor, I apologize profusely."

Igor was not laughing and kept shifting his position on the tired looking Ox.

"Your Majesty, I have a long road ahead of me and you are making fun as I must take this Ox instead of my dependable stallion."

"It's quite unfortunate that there are no other horses available. But an Ox, although slow, is quite dependable," said the King.

Igor shifts his weight again. "It's not the speed that concerns me; it's the comfort factor."

Slide is laughing hysterically. "I just can't see you sitting there for the four-to-six day ride to the stone quarry."

The King gives Slide the "look" and Slide stops laughing immediately. The King looks back at Igor sitting there on the Ox and then breaks out laughing uncontrollably again. "Slide is right. It's going to be a long ride. I take full responsibility for I have not provided you with the right tool for the job."

"I accept your apologies. However, I won't accept Slide's. I think he should come with me. We have plenty of Oxen and he can be there to inspect the quality of the stone right when it's lifted out of the quarry after the first rough cut."

Slide realizes now he might be in trouble. "Oh no, I don't think that's at all necessary."

"Igor, that's a splendid idea." He snaps his fingers and three stable hands start to prepare another Ox for the long trip. "Slide, it's really is a good idea. The two of you can talk construction and about our next project."

"Very well," said Slide. "If you wish."

Igor is now laughing. "Great! A companion."

"Now," said the King. "About this idea of having the right tool for the job. It seems to me that if one is to improve productivity, one has to have the right tools. I'm going to make it a top priority to survey all of the Kings men, as they say, and make sure they have the right tools to get their respective job done. That should take this Castle to the next level. What do you think?"

Igor contemplated the King's comments. "I think you're right. If we had horses, we would be there and back, and that would give us more time, which means we can get more work done."

"I agree," said Slide. "But can you give us another example?"

"Well, how about a company that requires its employees to use laptops, but won't buy them a mouse."

"I don't know about this laptop thing, but, to be honest, you can catch a mouse anywhere."

The King continues unperturbed by his dim-witted crew. "Other example might be the tools used at the quarry, or the tools of the craftsman, or the utensils needed to cook our food. It's endless."

"I'm starting to understand. But isn't that going to cost more money, your

Majesty?"

"Yes, yes. Good point. But see, there's another issue here. Besides making an employee more productive you instill in him confidence that I understand, and I'm here to help. This feeling of being appreciated will probably do more to increase productivity then anything else. It's always nice to be wanted. But it's always about the bottom line, but it's also not about the bottom line."

"Huh," said Slide and Igor in unison.

"See, it's about people. Treating people the right way will make them feel good and they will even work harder for you. It really is the right decision."

"You're a good King," said Igor. Slide agreed by nodding his head as he climbed aboard his Oxen.

"I'm glad that this has happened. I now have a new goal, one that will make my Kingdom even a better place." With that, he slapped the first Ox who started off in the direction of the gate, which lead to the moat drawbridge, which lead to the long, long road to the King's quarry.

As they traveled down the path, all they could hear in the background was the King's uproarious laughter. They also heard, "Beeee surrrrre toooooo wrrrrrite!" followed by more laughter.

Providing the right environment and tools for the job is an important concept. It means budgeting money appropriately and being willing to invest in your employees. This becomes part of the financial projection to include replacing outdated software and hardware, and where do you find this – in the business plan.

STORY #38
Sticks and Stones

"SLIDE AND IGOR, HOW DO YOU DO YOUR ACCOUNTING?" asked the King.

The King, Slide Rule and Igor were watching heavily guarded men drag sacks of gold into a rather imposing vault.

"Seriously?" responded Slide Rule, owner of Building Blocks, Inc., the King's No. 1 architect.

"Yes, seriously," answered the King with a slight change in voice tone. "Let's go over here and sit down and watch."

"I don't keep track of anything," answered Slide cautiously.

"And you, Igor?"

"I, the proud owner of Moat Designs, Ltd., use the sticks-and-stones method."

"Sticks and stones? Really," said the King. "That's a good one. Tell me about it?"

"Well, it's not really a proven system but it's based upon keeping track of who owes me and what I owe by having sticks represent income and stones represent debt. It's based upon and old poem that goes like this. . ."

"Sticks and Stones,
May Break my Loans,
But Gold will Never Hurt Me."

"Hummmmm, catchy tune. I hope I don't fall asleep with that running around in my head. Well, I dare say you're further ahead of Slide over there, but you're both in the dark ages when it comes to accounting and how to use it," said the King. "I believe we should spend the afternoon talking about accounting and the one important point that everyone misses."

155

"All afternoon?" pouted Igor.

"Do you have any better place to be than to spend the afternoon with your King in another Master Class?"

"Nope, not me," stated Slide enthusiastically. "Count me in."

"Is there going to be a test?" asked Igor.

"Yes, definitely. It will be to your benefit to pay attention. First, when interpreting the income statement and balance sheets, what is the one thing everyone overlooks?"

"Not having an accounting system, I couldn't even begin to guess what is most overlooked," said Slide.

Igor followed suit. "Haven't a clue."

"Well, let me tell you, this is the secret to running a business and no one does it. Here it is . . . People look at financial statements and never stop to think about what the number actually means, or what created that number."

"Keep going. I'm going to need more information," said Igor.

"Okay. For example, usually my communications expense is right around sixty shilling per month. I just got my statement, I'm using the advanced clay tablet system, and the communication expense went up to ninety shillings last month. Now that's gigantic increase. So I asked the question, why did it go up so high?"

Igor squirmed in his chair. "Very interesting. If I could ask, what's included in your communication expense?"

"As your King I need to keep myself informed on what's going on around my Castle. So I have two groups of Knights that ride between distant Castles on a monthly basis delivering messages, and then reporting relevant news items that might be important to me and running my Castle."

"So, this expense jumped. Why?" asked Igor.

"I wanted to know the same thing. So I took it upon myself to look behind the number and find out what it means. I call this Checking Past Accounts. I queried each of my Knights and found out that one of my vendors had asked one group of Knights to add an extra five days on to their route to check on the status of the delivery of granite building blocks that had been ordered. Isn't that right Igor?"

Igor laid his head on the table with his arms over them. He was quite sure this was the last time he was going to be able to feel his neck.

"Igor?"

Igor got up, approached the King and bowed. "Your Majesty, please forgive me. I had no idea that it would increase your expenses. I will pay everything back."

"Wow. Cheating the King. That's a good one," said Slide.

"Igor, you're not in trouble. But I did have to pay for all those Knights on the road. That's what ran up the cost. I just wished you had come and told me. I actually thought it was a very creative solution on your part. The lesson here is important: When you see numbers on your financial statement that doesn't make any sense, ask what is behind that number. It will always lead you toward a more profitable business."

"Now, about that test." Groans from the group. "The test is for you to review your financial statements at the end of each month, as it will help you in numerous ways to manage your business."

"I'm very excited about this," said Slide. "I'm so impressed; I'm going to start an accounting system."

"Good for you Slide. Checking Past Accounts is one of the best things you can do to remain profitable. In fact, I'm so convinced I'm going to abbreviate it and put it after my name. From now on I'm going to be known as The King, CPA."

Your financial statements are part of your business plan as they are a reflection of your business. You should also have a proforma financial statement showing your estimate of income and expenses for the company projected out for the year. If you're in a growth mode and want to look at your business strategically, you might project everything out over five years. The financials are a scorecard; they'll point to areas in your business that needs attention.

STORY #39
Where Does It Hurt?

THE SMALL STONE BUILDING were part of the shops that surrounded the open square for market day. Everyone brought in their wares, homemade goods and other merchandise to trade and sell. Slide Rule of Building Blocks, Inc, the King's No. 1 architect, and Igor, the contractor for the Castle and owner of Moat Designs, Ltd. saw the King approaching.

"Good morning," the King said as he hailed them.

Slide and Igor saw the King, and waved. "Your Majesty, we were just on our way to have a morning cup of warm sour goat's milk. Would you join us? It would be our pleasure," said Slide.

"That would be perfect. I have just left my chiropractor," replied the King. "A chiropractor? What is that, if I may ask," Slide said.

"If you have never been to a chiropractor, then you've missed a lot." "What do they do?" asked Igor.

"Generally speaking, they make small adjustments to your body that makes you feel better."

"That doesn't sound good at all. Actually, it sounds like it will hurt," said Igor.

"Is that where they press on your spine, or move your neck around and you hear everything crack and pop?" asked Slide.

"Yes, that's it," said the King with a great deal of excitement.

"Well, I'm not going to see them. I won't even shake hands with a chiropractor. It's all too scary."

"Nonsense. You can learn a lesson from them."

"And what's that? What can I possibly learn from a chiropractor?" Igor questioned.

The King is all smiles. "A chiropractor finds out where you hurt by pressing and poking here and there."

"If they would stop poking, you would stop hurting," commented Slide.

"No, no, Slide. It doesn't work that way. My point is, step back and look at your business and ask yourself, where does it hurt?"

Igor considered the King's response. "My business doesn't hurt. It might lose money, but it doesn't hurt."

"If you are losing money, then your business is hurting," answered the King.

"Oh," Said Igor.

The King motions toward an uncomfortable looking bench and table. "Here, let's sit down for a while and enjoy our refreshments and we'll talk about this." Both Igor and Slide sat down with their King. Warm lumpy sour goat's milk was immediately served to them.

"Now, if I may, there are several ways to determine if your business hurts. The first is financial. Are you taking in less money then you are spending? Is your debt too high? Do you have the ability to secure capital, or credit, for larger projects?"

"Wow, you're right. That would tell us if our business is hurting, as you say," said Slide.

The King was in top form and proceeded with his Master Class. "Oh, but there's more. Customer service is critical. Are your customers happy? When was the last time you did a survey to determine whether you're actually providing the services they want? Maybe you're missing an opportunity and they're thinking of moving to a new architect or contractor, or whatever business you're in. That would eventually begin to really hurt your cash flow."

Igor is getting the point. "You're correct. If we looked at customer service as a way to determine if our business is hurting, we could possibly prevent the situation where we could lose a customer."

"What else should we be concerned with, your Majesty?" asked Slide.

"What about industry trends? Are you up to date on what is happening within your own industry? What if a new technology comes along and you can't compete?"

Igor raised his hand like he was in class. "So, my King. I have a question to ask, if I may?"

"By all means. Please."

"How can you go to a chiropractor and come away with these ideas about business?"

"Ahaaa, yes. The magic question. And I, your King, have the magic answer."

"Which is…?"

"I would like you and Slide to be my guests and have several sessions with my chiropractor. Then you will know the answer. You see, they are really interested in how you feel. They will help you to reduce your stress, and you'll feel great and energized when you leave. Because of this newfound energy you too will have answers to questions you have not even thought about. Even questions about business."

Slide was now nervous. "Ahaaaaa, that's not really necessary. I don't even want to know the questions."

"Nonsense. I, your King, and your biggest client, insist that you give the chiropractor a try."

Igor sees the writing on the wall. "Very well, we'll be happy to go."

Slide hits Igor in the arm.

The King ignores Slide. "One last question. How much water do you drink?"

Where do you hurt? That's the main question to ask about your
company. If you need cash flow, work on cash flow.
If you need to improve your Operations to improve efficiency,
then that's what you do. Just keep poking to find out where you hurt.
This is a basic business planning strategy.

PART III
MARKETING

The marketing plan is what you're going to do this year to support the business plan, and in turn, support the long-range objectives of the strategic plan. You can't stop marketing because there's not a business plan or a strategic plan in place, but a well thought out strategic plan will change in subtle ways the marketing of your company. A marketing plan can be embedded with a business plan, or it can be a separate document with the key points summarized in the main business plan. Business Development is a key part of marketing as marketing brings the company and the prospect together, and the business developer makes the sale.

THE BUSINESS PATH TO GROWTH AND PROFIT

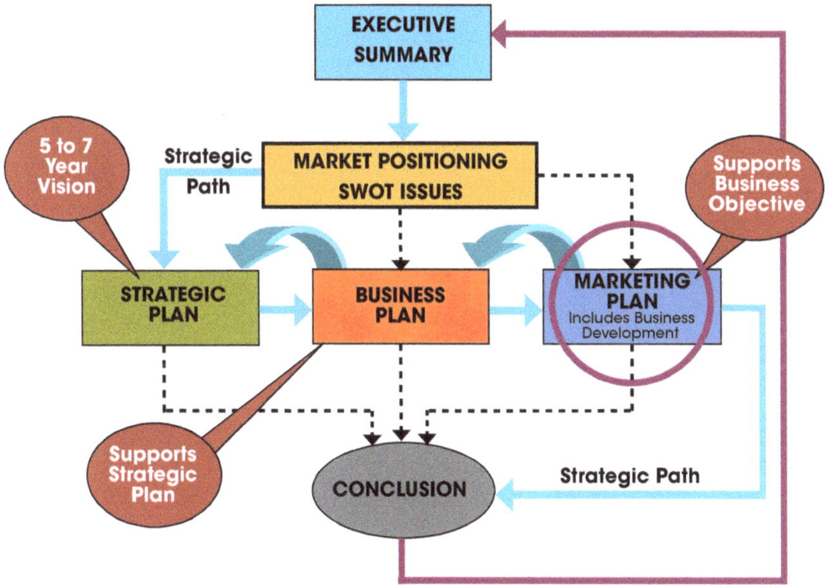

Fig. 3 The Business Planning Process - Marketing Plan

STORY #40
You Are What You Market

"SLIDE, PLEASE TELL ME ABOUT THE LAST PROPOSAL you submitted?" asked the King as he enjoyed his morning gruel with Igor and Slide Rule.

"So, it's like this," responded Slide of Building Blocks, Inc., the King's No. 1 architect. "The selection committee decided in their infinite wisdom they would have more face time with the other firm's principal because they have less work. So my competition wins the contract."

The King looked up holding his oversized spoon in mid air dripping gruel. "Why do they have less work?"

"Well, it appears they've lost several clients because they weren't paying attention to the details of the project. So in the minds of the owner this means the principal architect will have more time for his project."

"So, did they ever think to ask the question why your firm is so busy and their firm is losing work and as a consequence, has more time available? Ironically, it doesn't make any sense; they should want the architect that is not losing clients indicating the most success. Also, it goes without saying that the principal architect is going to be looking for more work, so it's all a white wash to get the job."

"I tried to suggest this to them, but I had to be careful as I didn't want to bad mouth the competition. That always comes back to haunt you."

"I would have told them everything and what happens, happens," said Igor of Moat Designs, Ltd. "A lost client is a lost client."

"I have the answer to this dilemma," said the King.

"I can hardly wait."

"The first problem is . . . ."

"The first problem? I have more then one problem?"

"Yes, you have lots of problems."

Igor laughs hysterically.

"So do you," said the King.

"Oh."

The King expounds in all his wisdom. "You are what you market. It's an issue of branding."

"The sheep hate that. The owner's aren't going to like it one bit," said Igor.

The King slowly turns his head toward Igor and stares at him. "Just listen. Branding is all about the perception of a company, or you are what you market. If the branding of a company is positioned on the personal service of a principal owner as part of that service, then everyone will expect that principal to be there. Likewise, if the firm has been positioned from the point of view of, say as an example, the quality of design that the 'firm' provides, then it may not be as important who shows up at the interview. For example, when a company is named after someone, like Berlinlinski Designs, it's very difficult to market that company without including the executives with that name. However, you two have smartly and wisely chosen to name your company Building Blocks and Moat Designs and now, probably by pure luck, you actually have an advantage in the market."

"It doesn't feel like an advantage," said Slide. "I just lost a deal because they don't think I'll be there."

"See, here is the bottom line, or as they say, where the drawbridge meets the dirt, everything is marketing. Everything! Branding is simply a marketing tactic. You lost the order because they didn't think you were going to be there, but, taking a step back, you really lost the order because of the perception of your company, and that's a marketing issue."

Igor pushes the bowl away after a satisfying morning meal of gruel and sour goat's milk. "So, what you're saying is, if Slide here had marketed his company so they wanted a 'Building Blocks' building, then it wouldn't matter who called on them?"

"Within reason, yes. People buy what you market."

"King, what do you market if I may be so bold to ask," stated Slide.

"My Kingdom," said the King with emphasis.

> "I market the security of our Knights in armor,
> To protect our hardworking farmers;
> The safety of the towering walls of stone,
> And the comfort of our Cathedral when alone.
>
> The firewood we cut to keep us warm,
> From the ever present building storms,
> That fills our rivers and streams,
> Providing us fresh water to redeem.
>
> The wild flowers that grow in the valley,
> And the summer showers that come as a finale;
> Haunting howls of the wolf at night,
> And the cheerful song of the rooster's morning rite,
>
> Best of all, I market a place to work and rest,
> And that we are all blessed."

"Wow, sire, you have spoken in the form of a sonnet," exclaimed Igor. "I'm truly impressed."

"You are what you market," replied the King.

What do you market? Do you design and build residential homes, or do you provide security for families? Do you sell cars, or do you market safety? Do you own a restaurant and sell food, or do you market a place where memories happen. You are what you market.

STORY #41
A Kind Gesture

IT WAS A VERY SERIOUS DISCUSSION. The King, Igor and Slide Rule were all huddled together and were talking in hushed tones.

"I lost another one," said Igor.

"You sound absolutely terrible," Slide said.

Slide Rule from Building Blocks, Inc. was the architect of the Castle, and Igor, from Moat Designs, Ltd. was the all around general contractor. They both served the King, for everyone served the King in some capacity, as that is why he was King.

"So, what are you going to do? What did you actually lose that has made you so depressed," asked the King.

"I was preparing to build a huge summer home. It was to be a very large project that would keep me busy until we started the new wing on the Cathedral. I lost it. They gave it to an outside contractor they had done business with in the past, even though I had more experience and was located right here near the Castle. I'm so depressed."

The King stood up and started to pace. "Do something nice for him."

"And how is that going to help me?" Igor said. Igor was so depressed even Slide the architect felt bad for him.

"First of all, forget about it!" the King said in his best Italian accent.

"I can't forget. I was counting on getting that project."

"Perhaps you can get a project from this company the next time?" said Slide.

Igor sat down completely spent and depressed. "There won't be a next time.

This was it."

"Trust me," said the King. "There's always a next time."

"So, tell me in all your wisdom, what shall I do?" asked Igor.

Slide was listening closely to the entire conversation. "Didn't you tell me that you were having a party next month?"

"Yes. That's true," replied Igor.

"So, the first thing you do is to take him off the list. The guys a loser," announced Slide.

The King interrupts the conversation. "No, that is not the right thing to do. It's absolutely the wrong thing to do."

"How so," asked Igor. Slide looked at Igor and shook his head.

"If you think there's work in the future with this client, and there always is, then you must put forth a response that shows him you're still here, and you hold no grudge about losing the project. You can do it quite indirectly. Send him a card inviting him to your special function and perhaps put him at a key table."

"I can't do that. He just selected another contractor."

The King announced in a stately manner, "There is nothing the renders a prospect more vulnerable then a kind gesture from the loser."

Slide now is getting interested. "I would never have thought of that."

"Yes, you're right Slide. You would have never thought of that. That's why I'm King. But see, think about it. It's a big market and you have time on your side. True, you lost this project. But so what? You had an opportunity to present your qualifications. Projects very often do not go to the most qualified; they often go to the one that has the best relationship. Worse yet, they are often awarded for completely the wrong reasons. And even worse, on hard bid situations, they often go to the company that is least qualified."

The King took a dramatic pause. "So, you invite them to your little party. It's in the corner of the Castle with the spectacular view where everyone wants to be, and everyone wants to come because of the food. They get the invitation and they are humbled. They awarded the project to a competitor and yet you still offer them excusive seats at your party. You'll make more progress in developing the relationship this way than anything else you can do. Now they feel vulnerable, and also sorry that they didn't select you. On top of that, you can do this with every project you lose that you really wanted. Some of them will be turned around."

"Wow," said Slide.

"You're right again," said Igor.

"I'll tell you what; I'll help you demonstrate my point."

"How so," Igor said.

"Have them sit at my table."

Never write a lost client off your list. Do the opposite. Constantly demonstrate to them that you care about their business.

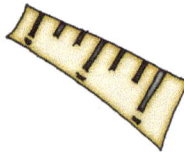

The King 🪑 McKenzie

STORY #42
Who Does He Know?

THE MARKETPLACE WAS CROWDED WITH VISITORS who came in on Saturday to sell their grains and other crafted home crafted wares. The Castle's marketplace was center of activity and the place to be.

Slide Rule of Building Blocks, Inc. had just met up with Igor of Moat Designs, Ltd. They were talking and enjoying the day when they saw the King and his normal entourage approach.

"Good to see you Slide and Igor. It's a great day for the market, don't you think?"

With a slight bow, Slide answers. "Yes, a great day. It gives me comfort knowing that all can visit and trade and enjoy the profits of the day."

"And you Igor?"

"Well, it's a great day. But it's too crowed for my taste."

"But it's the people and all their energy that makes this always a great occasion."

Just then a man that was in a hurry bumped into Igor. "See, that's what I mean. Its way too crowded, and too many people want to talk. But I've figured out a technique I use that helps me."

"What's that, if I may ask?"

"Well, just yesterday a decent looking fellow stopped to ask me questions when he found out I was the Castle's primary general contractor. Just then I saw someone I knew, and I grabbed him and made an introduction and then I just walked away. Problem solved!"

171

The King has listened intently to the story. "So, you basically abandoned him? Don't you think that's a little awkward for both of them?"

"No. Not at all. And besides, I don't get all tied down in all that chit chat?"

"Sounds like a good technique for a cocktail party," commented Slide.

"So Igor, let me ask you a question. Who did that person know that bumped into you yesterday?"

"I don't know who he knew, and I don't care."

"I sense big trouble," said Slide.

The King gives Slide a quick look that wipes the expression off of Slides face, and then he turns his attention to Igor. "You don't know who he knows? Is that what you're saying?"

"Yes. So what?"

"You don't know who he was. That's amazing."

"Why, what's the harm?"

"What if I told you there was a traveler in town who's visiting the different Castles in our area as he's going to be building a new Cathedral. He's looking for advisors who could help him ramp up the project and also provide the initial groundwork to make sure it's done right."

Igor is now devastated. "How . . . how would you know that?"

"You forget so easily I am your King."

"Oh right. I guess I made a big mistake."

"I'd say it was enormous," said Slide.

The King turns to Slide. "He was also looking for an architect."

Slide is now unhappy and slugs Igor in the arm. "Idiot."

"Here, here. I will have both of you in chains before you can snap your fingers if you don't stop it. There is a lesson here. Please understand this one point – you never know who someone knows. It may appear to be an innocent and accidental meeting. But what if that person could actually be in a position to help you? What if they had contacts that could a make a difference in your life?"

Igor was truly devastated. "You're right. I did the wrong thing. What a missed opportunity. It might have been the perfect project I've been waiting for."

"It could have been a great design commission," Slide said.

"Good. I see that both of you have learned your lesson. Now I would like to invite you to dinner in my chambers tonight."

"What's the occasion?" Slide asks.

"I have invited a guest. A traveler if you will, that's looking for input on a Cathedral he's going to build. I invite you as my guests to enjoy the evening and my company. Would you like to attend my little gathering?"

"I speak for Igor on this one. Yes, we would be pleased to come. And one more thing?"

"What is that?"

"You really are a good King."

It's true. You don't know who someone else knows. As an example, I'm two people away from the Pope, one person away from almost every Hollywood movie star, one person away from Al Pacino, and in fact, I personally know a Princess that works at a Starbucks®.

STORY #43
Leo Tolstoy and Architecture

"WHY ARE WE THE ONLY ONES WITH PROBLEMS," Igor said to Slide Rule and the King as the left the job site. Igor was owner of Moat Designs, the King's No. 1 contractor, while Slide Rule of Building Blocks, Inc., was the King's No. 1 architect.

Slide agreed with Igor. "I hear that other projects at other Castles don't have any problems, at least not like we run into. We can't get the craftsman; the soil is bad; the timbers for the rafters are a month out; and we ran into a bad batch of granite. It's just one thing after another."

The King sighed, and sat down. All you two do is complain!"

"Usually about each other. But this time, we're in total agreement. We both have a lot of problems." Slide said.

Igor nodded his head.

"It only seems that way," the King said.

"But I never hear any of our competitors have problems. It just feels like we're the only ones who do."

"Ahaa, you're missing a big point here that will make this whole problem go away."

"What is that may I ask?" Igor said.

"Leo Tolstoy wrote…"

"Leo Tolstoy? Are you kidding me? Who in the world is Leo Tolstoy?"

"He'll be a great writer one day," the King promised.

"Oh, I know. It's one of those future things. But we're talking about construction. It cannot possibly apply."

"Leo Tolstoy wrote about the human condition," said the King said.

Slide shakes his head in total disbelief. "I have no idea why we have these conversations."

The King now is in his full glory. "I was simply making an observation that will help you. And if it doesn't help you, since I am your King, you will like it anyway."

Igor ponders the moment. "Go ahead. I can hardly wait. If I don't hear it, I won't be able to sleep all night."

"Really?" Slide questioned.

Igor shot Slide a look.

"Oh, I see. Got it. Satire."

The King interrupts. "Well, here's the quote."

> "*Every man, knowing to the smallest detail all the complexity of the conditions surrounding him, involuntarily assumes that the complexity of these conditions and the difficulty of comprehending them are only his personal, accidental peculiarity, and never thinks that others are surrounded by the same complexity as he is.*" (The thoughts of Count Alexei Kirillovich Vronsky in Anna Karenina by Leo Tolstoy).

"You're so deep," said Slide.

Igor's interest is peaked. "Can you run that past me again?"

The King read it again, slowly emphasizing the last phrase.

"So," Slide says, "what you're saying is even if we have problems, it's the nature of the construction environment that others, just like us, also have problems, and some even worse than ours?"

"Right."

"So how does this help us?"

"It gives us perspective and depth. It allows us to focus on minimizing our challenges in an effort to build a better project faster, and eventually, take even a greater part of the market share away from our competitors who are building their own Castles."

"I see." Slide thought about this for a while. "So what you're saying is everyone always thinks their problems are greater then others. But basically we're all in the same boat."

"Maybe we should be building a bigger boat?" said Igor.

The King covered his face with his hands.

"I was just kidding."

The King shakes his head in total disbelief but continues on. "Everything is relative. All Castles have problems, some worse and some a lot less than we have. But the point is that problems are opportunities to shine in front of our clients. We can get more mileage by solving problems efficiently, and without complaints, than we could ever hope to imagine."

"So your Majesty, you're saying we should welcome these problems for it's how our client is really going to remember us." Igor asked.

"Yes, and if they remember us they will do two things: They will come back to us when they need more work, and they will refer us to others—all because we have problems on the job that we solve quickly and efficiently without complaints."

"You make everything sound so positive," said Slide.

"All good comes from positive thoughts and directed focused action."

"Who said that, Tolstoy?"

"No, I did, your King."

View a problem or a challenge as an opportunity to demonstrate your professionalism and dedication to get the job done right.

STORY #43
Communication Blunders

THEY WERE ALL LAUGHING VERY HARD. In fact, the King, Igor and Slide Rule could barely control themselves. Igor of Moat Designs, and Slide Rule of Building Blocks, Inc. were enjoying the hot day by cooling themselves off with their regular afternoon watered down wine.

"Oh, I've got something for you. Try this out — here's a line of copy from an advertising agency about what they do," the King announced as he broke into uncontrollable laughter.

"You have an agency?" responded Igor. "I am impressed."

"Both of you should have agencies to help you market. But let me read this to you. *'We are offering a one-two-three punch of behavioral planning and engagement mapping.'*"

More laughter ensued. "What could that possibly mean?" asked Slide. "It's all nonsense and mish-mash. I'm no longer impressed you have an agency!"

"Thankfully, this is not my agency." said the King. "But, that's my point. Companies get so tied up in their own vision of themselves; they forget what they sound like. People need to learn to communicate in plain English, and not try and impress one with austere sound bites of futuristic possible consequences laced with supportive alternates."

They all laughed along with the King at his clever satire.

"You're starting to sound like them. Maybe they work for a competing Castle. They could only help you," Slide said.

More laughter followed at Slide's observation.

The King unfolded another page. "Here's one from an architect."

Igor is now very happy. "Ha ha ha. This oughta be good."

The King reads. "`Although we incorporate state-of-the-art CAD computer design systems into our work, we specialize in unique one-of-a-kind facilities that combine excellent form with progressive function.`"

"What's CAD?" asked Slide.

"It's one of those future things. But look at what they're saying; the use of CAD has not hindered their ability to function as a unique designer. CAD, besides as an aid to increasing productivity, is all about giving the architect tools to help them visualize the building systems and to examine relationships in three dimension to help them design unique one-of-a-kind facilities. With CAD you get walkthroughs and perspectives from every angle. They don't get it; they should be saying CAD helps them as a unique designer. It's a huge blunder of enormous proportions. Doublespeak with no meaning."

Igor and Slide just shook their heads. The King, who appeared to be very happy with his watered down wine said, "Here's another one from a marketing company. *It will include developing a better understanding of established metrics, identifying their predictive capabilities and enhancing customer and prospect intelligence to improve a go-to-market strategy.*"

"Huh?" says Slide.

"How about this one? *They specialize in science translation, cross-border indicators, cross-disciplinary planning and environmental technical assistance to businesses with an increasing focus on sustainable tourism.*"

Igor chimes in. "Go to market strategies? Why don't they just go to the marketplace? It's every Sunday rain or shine. I don't get it."

More laughter.

The King sits back in his chair as he downs the last of his wine. "It's really quite amazing the kind of information that reaches out to the market. They're trying so hard to differentiate themselves from the competition, they come across as idiots. I can't imagine the conversations they had in their conference rooms as they created phrases that were actually published in prestigious construction and design related publications. As well as the B-to-B journals."

"Here's another one to reflect on. *'You have these different systems that do different things. It's a lot of work to get multiple systems to talk to each other.'*"

"I can't get my architect and contractor to talk to each other. How in the world am I going to get multiple systems to talk to each other?" said the King.

"So, what's the solution?" Igor asks.

"The solution is to never let wild and ambiguous marketing statements get out of your office. It's so much better to be clear and concise in your statements so that everyone understands what you're saying."

"Do you have an example?" asked Slide.

"Yes. Try this one out — Keep It Simple, Slide."

Author's Note: Years later this was changed to *"Keep It Simple, Stupid."*

Clearly, outbound marketing penetration strategies, coupled with cross-mapping multiple system communication alternatives, while pushing the boundaries of projected metrics, translates into progressive functional design-based prospect oriented focused solutions and engagement contracts with predictive capabilities.

STORY #45
It's All in the Name

THE KING WAS ENJOYING THE SUNNY MORNING at the marketplace. It was Saturday and for miles around farmers and craftsman brought in their crops and handcrafted wares and other assorted items to trade at the market. You could trade or purchase just about anything, and the King was proud as this was the center of his Kingdom's economy. Food, drink, games and happy hard working people were doing business and having fun.

The King had decided to greet people as they entered and took up a location just outside the Moat and Drawbridge where he could greet the people coming and going. Slide Rule of Building Blocks, Inc. the King's No. 1 architect joined him along with Igor, from Moat Designs, Ltd. who was the general contractor for the Castle.

"So, today is a good day. I feel alive, well and happy," said the King.

"I agree with you," said Igor as Slide also nodded his head in agreement. They were all enjoying the activity of the morning. It was a good day for the King and his Castle.

"Where are my pets," asked the King. Everyone starts looking around.

The King stands up and starts to call his beloved pets. "Here Ambien. Here Ambien."

"If I may say something, your Majesty. That is a strange name for a pet," commented Slide.

"It's the name I gave him." As if on cue, a rather sleepy looking mixed breed dog wanders up to the King. He barks once and lies down at the Kings feet and falls fast asleep. "This dog does nothing but sleep all day long. I can't figure it out."

The King continues his quest. "Here Viagra. Here Viagra."

181

Just then a very lively and happy Labrador Retriever bounds into the middle of the group panting and barking. Viagra was apparently very happy with life.

"This dog never stops moving," said the King. "And boy, can he fetch."

"That's also a strange name for a pet," stated Slide.

The King raised his eyebrows and looked at Slide. "Are you questioning my ability to name my pets?"

"Oh no," your Majesty. Nothing of the kind," responded Slide who now was a bit worried that he has overstepped his bounds.

Slide stood up and bowed. "You have one more pet. What's his name and I'll help you find him."

"Valium," replied the King.

"Here Valium. Here Valium," yelled Slide.

Everyone waited and after about ten minutes of calling out for Valium a very large Basset Hound ambles into the group, sits down and stares into space with his head cocked to one side.

"I never can get that dog excited about anything," commented the King.

Igor had been watching and he too stood up and bowed. "Your Majesty, if I may ask, you have shown us a great deal of creativity in naming your beloved pets. Is there a message there; something we can take with us to make our lives better?"

The king smiled. "Igor, I'm so proud of you. Please sit down and listen."

As Igor turned to sit down, he smirked at Slide for he knew he had gotten a point from the King.

"Yes, there is a message here. You see, most people think that only artists and craftsman are creative. But in reality, everyone can be creative no matter what they do. Being creative is the lifeblood of business; it's what creates new commerce; it can develop new relationships or cause you to look at the old way of doing something, and find a new way that is better, cheaper and much more attractive. Likewise, being creative is what teaching is all about. Learning new ways to instill the magic of learning with the youngsters is as important as building this Castle. Being creative is the source of growth no matter what you do. It is the essence of marketing."

"I had never thought of it that way," said Slide. I'm guilty of only thinking of artists and architects at being creative. You're right. Do you have any last words of wisdom?"

"Creativity is the source of all business energy. But the real secret is that being creative makes the world that much more interesting, if not life itself."Creativity is more than the arts; real creativity is how you solve problems, deal with people, and manage your business. Creative people stay in business, non-creative people go out of business.

STORY #46
Marketing Noir

"SO IGOR, WHAT WOULD RICK BLAINE DO?" the King asked. Igor of Moat Designs, Ltd., and Slide Rule of Building Blocks, Inc., the King's No. 1 architect were sitting with their King in the lobby of an advertising agency. The King was planning the Castle's next year's marketing campaign to draw in more farmers and craftsman to his Market Square.

"Rick who?" replied Igor.

"Blaine."

Igor thought for a second. "Don't know him."

"Humphrey Bogart played him in Casablanca. He was the owner and operator of Rick's Café American."

"Oh, that Rick Blaine! Like, have you been drinking, or are you doing one of your future things because the author, *(Hi, I'm the Ron the author)*, can't figure out another way to get into this article. Why did you think of that?"

The King pointed toward the block wall showing a Casablanca poster.

"Oh. But why are you showing me that?" Igor got up and took a closer look at the poster.

"Because I have coined the phrase 'Marketing Noir' to describe what you do," The King replied.

"I'm afraid to ask, but what does 'Marketing Noir' mean? And where do you get these ideas?"

Slide nodded in agreement.

"Noir means 'of or relating to a genre of crime literature featuring tough, cynical characters and bleak settings.' "

"Are you saying our offices are bleak and we are cynical, tough characters?" said Slide.

"No."

"Are you saying you are that lone figure that, through despair and injustice, seeks out future projects for the Castle through marketing and business development in heroic fashion?"

"Yes."

Igor was stunned. "You're kidding, right?"

The King stood up, and Igor and Slide then knew another Master Class had just started. "Actually, no. Think about it. What I mean is, so many executives and managers in all types of businesses do not recognize that marketing and business development are an integral part of a business. It's part of the entire infrastructure that makes a business work. So many times when business becomes slow, the marketing budget is cut, and the marketing employees are let go. The financial officer says, *'Why don't you just cut marketing? Apparently it's not working and it's costing you a fortune. You can save a lot of money and move it over to the bottom line.'*"

"Maybe, just maybe, it's the financial officer trying to protect their position?

Seems to me you could easily outsource those tasks," commented Igor.

The King looked at Igor. "You know, I had never even thought of that."

"The same goes for Human Resources," said Slide.

"Wow, I am duly impressed. You have given me something to think about. Seriously. This could change everything."

Slide raised his hand, and the King nodded toward him. "Marketing is cut all the time because in business, when there's no money, there's no money. It's the only solution."

Igor agreed nodding his head.

"You're right. But the point is, by managing using the business planning process, you have advance warnings of a decline business, and that allows you to tweak marketing and business development so getting to the point of a disaster should never happen."

Slide agreed. "I understand. We've made a real commitment to marketing. Sure, everyone markets in some way, but we've made a very large commitment to actively communicate our value message to clients, prospects, allies and the usual suspects to avoid getting in trouble. In this way, we can bring attention to the services we offer relative to how we can solve their problem and save them money at the same time. That makes us different; it means that because we are committed to success and we're in for the long haul, we have become like one of those Humphrey Bogart characters."

"So 'Marketing Noir' means we conceptually have become that dark character who moves through the shadows to get the job done and always is ready for more," Igor said.

The King is getting excited. "Good for you Igor and Slide. But there's more. It also means we have passion for what we do. It means we have a commitment to do it the right way regardless of the economic situation. We don't give up. We continually market and continually present our services. It's the passion for what we do that makes us different. It is 'Marketing Noir.'"

"Wow, you watch movies from a completely different perspective than I do!" said Igor.

In there someone in your company that matches the "Marketing Noir" characterization?

STORY #47
Value and Price

IGOR WAS TOTALLY DEPRESSED. Igor was the owner of Moat Designs, the castles main contractor.

"Igor, why are you so depressed," inquired Slide Rule who headed up Building Blocks, Inc.

"The work is not coming in. I'm taking projects at cost just to keep people on the payroll."

The King, who had just walked up and had overheard the conversation, nodded his head in sympathy. "You must be losing money?"

"I'm losing money and I'm trying to generate Change Orders to make a profit. Even though I have work I'm getting deeper in debt. I need to make more money on the bottom line."

"Move the line," responded Slide with a smile at his clever and obvious solution.

The King looked at Slide. "You're an idiot." The King rested his hand on Igor's shoulder. "I think I can help you."

Igor brightened. "Your Majesty. You pay me what I'm worth. It's my other clients who don't pay me what I need to charge."

"Then you need to educate them. You need to communicate price and value relationships. Particularly you Slide. You lose money on everything you touch."

"We're all ears," said Slide. Igor nodded his head in agreement.

"Well first, let me recite something to you written by John Ruskin. He said the following:

187

The King 🪑 McKenzie

*"It is unwise to pay too much, but it is worse to pay too little.
When you pay too much, you lose a little – that is all.
When you pay too little, you sometimes lose everything,
because the thing you bought was incapable of doing the thing
you bought it to do. The common law of business balance
prohibits paying a little and getting a lot – it cannot be done!
If you deal with the lowest bidder, it is well to add something
for the risk you run; and if you do that, you will have
enough to pay for something better."*

"That's really deep," said Igor.

"But it makes sense," said the King excitedly. "Think about it, '"It is unwise to pay too much, but it is worse to pay too little.' Now that really sums it up. In construction many people who are not experienced, as well as many attorneys believe that the project should always go to the lowest bidder. Their position is if they made a mistake, or purposely bid low to capture the job, then that's their problem, not yours. Then everything goes crazy when someone starts to lose money and they start pointing fingers at each other. It's a nightmare."

Igor was listening intently, and then spoke showing his frustration at not being paid for what he was worth. "You're right. The old adversarial roles start to kick in when someone starts to realize they're going to loose money. Everyone starts to look for ways to cut corners and transfer some of the loss to the other subcontractors."

"And the beat goes on...." said the King.

"What?"

"Never mind. It's an expression. Then Ruskin says . . . .

*"When you pay too much, you lose a little – that is all.
When you pay too little, you sometimes lose everything,
because the thing you bought was incapable of doing
the thing you bought it to do."*

"How many times have we seen that scenario played out?"

"Many times your Majesty. Are you suggesting we communicate this to our clients?"

"Yes, by all means. But you need to communicate in terms of the difference between value and price."

"You get what you paid for is another way of saying the same thing," said Slide.

"Yes, true. Very good Slide," said the King who then continued with his wisdom. "And then … get this, Ruskin says. . . ."

> *"The common law of business balance prohibits paying
> a little and getting a lot-it cannot be done!'*

"I ask you, when was the last time you paid a little and got a lot. Never. It doesn't work that way. And yet in construction, that's what happens."

"Who promotes that kind of thinking," asked Slide.

"It's human nature to pay as little as you can for what ever service or product you want. But it's the smart business person that knows that paying the right price means he will in the end, get a lot more for his money. Just listen to his last statement."

"If you deal with the lowest bidder, it is well to add something for the risk you run; and if you do that, you will have enough to pay for something better."
"How many times has someone had to dip deeper in their pocket to fix something that has just been fixed? That's why in the private sector corporations will throw out the high and the low bid and look at the middle grouping. This is done on the theory that the high and low bidders are the ones with the biggest mistakes."

"So, what's the next step?" asked Igor.

"Yes, the infamous next step. What you need to do is to prepare some material that's used in your proposal to both directly and subliminally communicate value and price. It might go something like this."

"The pricing of Moat Designs, Ltd is based upon experience. We are neither the lowest price nor the highest price. Our pricing is determined to insure that we can provide exactly what we say we are going to provide without any 'change order' games or buying out the cheapest subcontractor and then forcing them to perform with threat of lawsuit. In the end, you save money for we get the job done, and historically or record shows, under budget with a cost savings coming back to you. We're open book, which means you know where all the money is going. There are no hidden mark-ups. You know everything. There are no secrets; we are your partner and we are here to make you successful. Think of us as your in-house construction company. We are rewarded for fairness and professionalism and take our responsibilities seriously."

Your Majesty," said Igor. "I have only one question."

"I will be happy to answer."

"Will you go to the next presentation with me?"

The real secret to winning more proposals is to learn what the owner considers as 'value' as different owners or companies, will have different ideas of value. When you learn this you have a real competitive advantage.

STORY #48
Another Day, Another Shilling

"ANOTHER DAY, ANOTHER SHILLING," said the King as he slumped down on the tree stump in the shade of the Castle's Pub.

"That's easy for you to say," said Igor, the King's No. 1 moat contractor and all around builder.

"And what do you mean by that," inquired the King. "Are you saying I don't work for a living?"

"Oh no, your Majesty. I am humbled by the amount of work you do," replied Igor.

Slide Rule, the chief architect of the King's Castle and owner of Building Blocks, Inc. walked up and also slumped down on a short stool next to him. Slide yawned. "I didn't get much sleep last night. A round of watered down wine for everyone," Slide announced.

An applause broke the hot muggy air, and Slide suddenly realized that everyone in the Pub thought they were getting a free drink.

"But, but . . . ."

"It's okay," said the King. I have you covered." He waved his hand with a flourish and received a round of applause in gratitude for his kindness on the hot summer day.

Igor was also beat. "All this work. When will it ever end?"

The King looked at Igor and then at Slide. "Work never ends. It's the way it is. You know what Ellen Goodman said, don't you?"

"No," responded Igor.

Slide covered his eyes. "Here we go again."

"What's that supposed to mean?" asked the King rising out of his chair.

"Nothing, nothing at all," replied Slide hurriedly covering his potential gaff, his career and his life.

"Goodman, a Pulitzer Prize winning columnist said . . . ."

> *"Work is getting dressed in clothes that you buy for work, driving through traffic in a car that you are still paying for, in order to get to the job that you need so you can pay for the clothes, car and the home that you leave empty all day in order to be able to afford to live in it."*

"What's a car?" asked Igor.

"It means cart. They forgot to put the letter 't' at the end."

"Oh. So now it makes some sense. To me it says, if you don't work, you won't need the clothes, and you also won't need the cart."

"So what would you do all day, Slide?" asked Igor.

"I'd sit around and drink watered down wine."

"How would you pay for it?" asked the King.

Slide thought about it. "Looks like we're back to square one."

"You're both idiots," announced the King.

Slide leaned forward. "But think about it, your Majesty. You work hard all day, every day. You are a 24/7 King. What's the point with all this work if we're just paying as we go? What's the point that I design a good building, and Igor builds them well? Just look at Igor and I. All we do is work."

"Good question. The answer is different for everyone. See, the purpose of work is to make a better place for everyone. Doing your job well is your reward."

"Doesn't feel like it?" said Igor.

Slide nodded his head in agreement.

The King thought for a moment. "Maybe there's a greater purpose to all of this. Perhaps it's what one thinks about when they're working, and what one does with their free time when they're not working that makes the difference."

"Meaning?" asked Igor.

"Meaning, your life's work is also about what you think about and what you do to help your fellow man. There is more to life then getting up and going to work, and coming home and flopping down on your feathered bed to watch the drama of the setting sun. It's about what you do when you're not working; it's about helping those less fortunate; it's about doing your life well."

"I thought this was a column on marketing and planning?" asked Slide.

"It is. The best marketing one can do is to help your fellow man. The best planning you can do is to help plan for that. The real work is becoming a better person. The best you can do at work can only be judged by you, at night, when you close your eyes and go to sleep."

Slide yawned. "Your Majesty, I don't sleep that well at night."

"There you have it. Now you know how to go to sleep at night, every night." You have a choice. Do your best and help your clients, friends and associates more than what they expect, and you will sleep every night.

STORY #49
Prepping for Presentations

"I CAN MEET YOU ANYTIME THIS WEEK" said Igor of Moat Designs, Ltd. "Slide Rule and I are giving a joint presentation for some new business next week, so our agenda is wide open."

Slide Rule, of Building Blocks, Inc. nodded his head in agreement. "Anytime, your Majesty. Anytime."

The King looked at them in amazement. "What kind of presentation are you going to be giving?"

"It's a design/build proposal to construct a massive rock wall that runs along the river. Slide's going to design it and I'm going to build it. It will provide a focus point for the Castle but the owner's real reason is to keep the sheep out of the riverbed."

"So this would be a good commission?"

"Oh yes. It would provide Slide with some design and engineering work and it would keep me busy until the fall. Why do you ask?"

"Because you said you have nothing to do this week."

"That's correct."

"What about practicing for the presentation?"

"Nah. We like to wing it. It keeps us on our feet and keeps the blood pumping if you know what I mean."

"No, I don't know what you mean. Let me ask you this, how many of these types of presentations do you win?"

"Almost none."

"Uh Oh." said Slide.

Igor looked at Slide and then the King. "Uh Oh."

"Yes," replied the King. I think you get my message. My Master Class is now in session. Let's talk about the different ways companies can prep for presentations. You both have the time, I take it?"

"Yes, your Majesty" responded Slide and Igor in unison.

"Okay. Now there are five different techniques for preparing for presentations. Obviously, your technique, which we will call the **I Don't Want It Technique,** is the least desirable. Number two is the **Read It Before We Get There** technique which means you read the instructions for the invitation to present just before you get there."

"We've used that one quite often."

"Number three is the **Just Use What We Used Last Time and Change the Name** technique."

"Wow," said Igor. "We've also used that technique."

"Now, the fourth technique is getting better. This is where one person does their homework, and does research on the company they're presenting too, and then encourages various strategy meetings to practice their presentation, but it never happens. At least that person is ready regardless of the rest of the team. I call this one the **I'm Ready and You're Not** technique.

"We had a business developer working for us at one time, and that describes him perfectly. He was always trying to get us to prepare for the meeting. Now I understand what he was doing," said Slide.

"Yes, those architect business developers are by far the best. Now, the very best technique is referred to as **I Want the Business and I'm Willing to Work for It** technique. In this scenario the presentation team sits around a table and strategizes what it will take to win, regardless of the competition?

195

They compile a competitive intelligence report as well as what the 'word on the street' is saying. They develop a customized presentation that includes the opening, the middle and the close based upon research, stressing the prospect more than yourself. They figure out ways to engage the prospect in talking about their true needs and wants. You want the prospect to talk so you can interweave their hot buttons into your presentation. On top of that you actually role-play the presentation to get comfortable with the material before you actually present."

"Wow," commented Slide.

"There's more. The goal of this approach is to talk more about the prospect and how you can help them, than to talk about your company and yourself. In this technique there is rehearsal and planned objectives from the time you walk into a meeting until you leave. Even what you are carrying and who carries it into the room is planned out in advance."

"Wow, that's a lot of work," Slide says.

"I've got news for you," said the King.

"News?"

"Yes, fast breaking news. Prepping for a presentation the right way which includes role modeling and rehearsing the opening and closing lines, where you actually ask for the order, is a lot less work in the long run, if you don't have any work at all."

"Meaning?"

"Have you ever been to a Going Out of Business Sale?"

"No."

"Well, if you don't present the very best that you can, you'll be the one going out of business, and let me tell you, it's a lot of work."

Don't pretend to want the business. Show the prospect you want their business and why your company is the best choice.

STORY #50
Three Shilling Swill

"MARKETING, MARKETING, MARKETING," exclaimed Slide Rule of Building Blocks, Inc, the King's No. 1 architect.

"Same here," commented Igor, of Moat Designs, the contractor for the Castle.

"Well, that's the first positive thing I have heard you two say," said the King of the Castle. The three of them were enjoying a glass of wine down by the river. They sat on a blanket and were quite comfortable.

Slide and Igor exchanged glances, and then looked at the King. The King had misinterpreted what they had said, as they were really complaining about marketing.

All three sipped their wine in the afternoon sun, which was making them sleepy. Igor dozed off first, and then Slide closed eyes and nodded his head while holding his wine glass at a dangerous angle. The King, who had been pretending to be sleepy, opened his eyes and looked at his top construction advisors.

The King waved toward his Knights who rolled a 500 lb. canon over and placed it between the King's two sleeping advisors. The canon was pointed across the river, and when all was clear, the King gave the signal, and the fuse was lit. Everyone ran for cover.

The canon exploded with such a force the ground shook. As the smoked cleared they could see Slide and Igor clutched together trying to hide under the blanket absolutely terrified. All the Knights in Shinning Armor were laughing at them.

The King walks up. "So, do I have your attention now?"

"What did you say," said Igor.

"Do I have your attention now," yelled the King.

"Yes, your Majesty. We must have dozed off."

"The same here," replied Igor who was visibly shaken. "Are we at war?"

"No. I was just trying to make a point. It's the middle of the afternoon, and you're sleeping on the job."

"We both apologize," said Igor.

The King snapped his fingers. "Wine for all of us." He then turned toward both of them. "Let's see, you were making comments about marketing."

Slide, quite shaken from the ordeal, sat down. "Yes, it's never ending. Always another campaign."

The King brightened. "What you need is a campaign that can run for twelve to eighteen months."

"Is there such a thing?"

"Certainly. Consider the wine you're drinking."

Slide swirled the wine around in his glass, took a sip, swished it around in his mouth and spit it out as a fine expert would do. "It appears to be a good wine, fresh, full body."

"It's called Three Shilling Swill."

"Really," said Igor. "I've heard of it. In fact, people are coming from all over to give it a try. They usually buy several cases of the wine just for the novelty of it."

Slide took a sip. "Actually, it's good and it's cheap. This should really get people interested because everyone is talking about it."

The King laughed his merry robust laugh. "Yes, you're right. In fact, Three Shilling Swill is going to be so popular that someday it's going to be compared to Two Buck Chuck, which is one of the greatest marketing promotions ever."
"So, what's your point?"

The King got up and started to pace. "My Master Class is now in session. Here's my point. You should be using a matrix of marketing tactics, such as direct mail, white papers, social media, blogs, advertisement, principal speeches, lunches, sporting events, and websites to name a few."

"There's no way we can afford to do all of that," said Slide.

"Good Slide. That's my major point."

Slide beams at the compliment.

"You can't do all of them, but what you can do is go to your experienced business developer marketing expert and work out a matrix of possibilities based upon a budget."

"My B.D. guy did that and we just pretty much ignored everything he said."
"How's business," asked the King.

Igor shrugged his shoulders.

"That's what I thought. Anyway, some of these campaigns can be short and targeted, while other ones, like Three Shilling Swill, can take place over a longer period of time because it's clever and draws attention. It will get people talking about your company, and that's what you want."

"What's the first step?" asked Slide.

"The first step is to sit down with your marketing and business development team and actually talk about business. In these hard economic times, they take it seriously. You should too."

"Sounds good," Slide. "We'll both give it a try."

The King 🪑 McKenzie

"Marketing is a blast," said the King who laughed merrily with his Knights of the Roundtable.

You cannot predict what marketing tactic is going to attract what buyer, or interest what prospect. You need to measure the results as to cost and response. Test! Test! Test!

Note: "$2-Buck-Chuck" marketing phenomena was marketing through Trader Joes and is considered one of the best marketing campaigns ever.

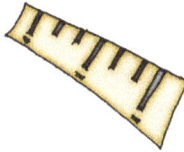

STORY #51
Blah, Blah, Blah

THE KING, IN ALL HIS MAJESTY, walked into the garden court of his Castle. Waiting for him were his top two advisors, Slide Rule of Building Blocks, Inc, the King's No. 1 architect, and Igor, of Moat Designs, the contractor for the Castle.

"So, my students," as he liked to call them. "I see you're here for today's lesson in my Master Class. Today's topic is Concise Copy Writing, and in particular, blah blah blah blah. Blah blah. Blah blah blah and blah. Blah blah blah blah. Therefore, it's imperative that blah blah. blah. Blah blah blah blah."

Slide yawned.

"Slide, do you have a problem with marketing?"

"Marketing, marketing, marketing," exclaimed Slide. "It's all I hear about."
"Did you do your lessons?"

"No. They were way to long to read."

"I agree with you. In fact you make a good point," replied the King.

Slide beamed at the praise and turned toward Igor who grimaced at him.

"Today's lesson is there is too much copy in today's marketing world. Marketing copy should be to the point and get the message across as quickly as possible. Blah blah. Blah blah blah and blah. Blah blah blah blah. Blah blah. Blah blah blah and blah. Blah, blah blah blah. Blah blah, Blah blah blah blah. Blah blah."

"Does this mean a shorter class," asked Igor.

The King continued, ignoring Igor. "In fact, some people break down copy into four distinct parts, and they often can appear in a different order depending upon the situation."

"First, there needs to be a Unique Selling Proposition that immediately attracts your prospects attention. The USP, as it is referred to, is directed at who buys your product or services, and why your solution is different and will help them solve their problem or need. Blah blah blah and blah. Blah blah blah blah. Blah blah. Blah blah blah and blah. Blah blah blah blah. Blah blah. Blah blah blah and sometimes blah. Blah blah blah blah. Traditionally this leads to blah, blah blah."

"Blah blah blah and blah. Many people have a problem with this, So, my recommendation is to blah blah blah blah, and blah blah. blah. Blah blah blah blah. Blah blah. Blah blah blah and blah. Blah blah blah and blah. Blah blah blah blah. Often, blah blah."

"Blah blah blah and blah. Remember this, as it's important to blah blah and blah. Blah blah blah blah. Blah blah. Blah blah blah and blah. Blah blah blah blah. Blah blah. Blah blah blah and blah. Blah blah blah blah."

"Second, you should demonstrate that what you're selling addresses the needs and wants of your target market. Blah blah blah and blah, blah blah blah blah."

"Third, there needs to be a call to action to take advantage of the offer so they can enjoy the benefits which solves their problem. Blah blah blah and blah. But I will note that blah blah blah blah. Blah. Blah blah blah blah. Blah blah. blah blah blah and blah. Blah blah blah blah."

"And fourth, include testimonials in the copy or the ad. This is important as it is better to have other people talking about your company and services than you. Blah blah blah and blah. Hardly a marketing day goes by where blah blah blah. Until that critical time arrives, I suggest blah blah. blah. Blah blah blah blah. Blah blah. Blah blah blah and blah. Blah blah blah blah. Blah blah blah blah.

Igor and Slide look at each other.

The King continues. "Blah blah blah and blah. Hence, realize that blah blah blah blah. Blah blah blah blah. Blah blah. Blah blah blah and blah. Blah blah blah blah. Blah blah. Blah blah blah and blah. Blah blah blah blah. Often, blah blah. It's all about being concise. That's the number one copywriting rule."

"Also, don't confuse copy writing with content writing where you're explaining something that the reader needs to understand in order to do something. Blah blah blah and blah. Blah blah blah blah. Blah blah blah blah. Blah blah. Blah blah blah and blah. Blah blah blah blah."

"One last important point. Blah blah blah blah. Blah blah. Blah blah blah and blah. Blah blah blah blah. Blah blah. Blah blah blah blah. Blah Blah. Blah blah blah and blah. You can quote me."

"Blah blah blah. Blah blah. blah blah blah and blah. Blah blah blah blah. Blah blah. Blah blah blah and blah. Blah blah blah blah. Often, blah blah. Igor and Slide look at each other.

Finally, Slide steps forward. "Your Majesty, we're thankful for your wisdom. We will put this to good use immediately. Our copy will be short, and to the point."

"Excellent," responded the King.Blah blah blah and blah. "But one more important point. Marketing is a changing environment as the prospects needs and wants change. So, you must, and I want to be clear, you must always update and freshen your material on a regular basis. Therefore, blah blah blah blah and blah blah. Blah blah blah blah. Blah blah. Blah blah blah blah. Blah blah. Blah blah blah and blah. Blah blah blah blah. Often, this leads to blah blah and finally, and you guessed it, blah, blah and blah."

Be brief.

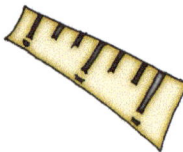

204

STORY #52
What Good Would That Do?

THE KING ENTERS HIS CHAMBERS. Slide Rule, of Building Blocks, Inc. the lead architect for the Castle, and Igor, the owner of Moat Designs, Ltd. bow to their King as he takes his seat.

The King nods his head toward his two friends.

"Your Majesty, if we may, Igor and I have come up with several creative marketing tactics. We would like to indulge you for a few minutes and run them past you. We're excited about marketing and are eager to launch our plans."

"Very well. I'm interested. Please, proceed."

Slide takes center stage. "First, we have decided that Social Media marketing is not going away, and we're proposing a multi-level attack. We want to take whatever news item we have and first put it on LinkedIn, and then on Facebook, and then Tweet it. At the same time an electronic press release is sent to our clients, prospects and our industry news sources. Our web site will be simultaneously updated, but even more important; the web site will refer to our blog that will have white papers for downloading. We want to get people talking. What do you think?"

"What good would that do?" said the King.

Igor and Slide looked at each other somewhat baffled by the King's sarcastic response.

"Well," said Igor, "Let's try another one."

"Very well, proceed," said the King.

"This tactic is to develop a business letter campaign. Now this sounds old fashioned, but consider this; since there is all of this digital marketing going on, a future thing I might add, the old-fashioned business letter is still a good way to get our message right in front of the prospect. We will use our letter-head and business envelopes to avoid looking like a mass produced direct mail piece. Each letter will be signed so it's personalized, and in the letter will be an offer to help them in some manner, such as a free on-site survey. If we can get in front of them we have a better chance at making a sale. It will compliment or Social Media campaign. We're flanking our prospects for the best hit possible. What do you think?"

"What good would that do?" said the King.

Igor looks at Slide Rule completely baffled by the King's response. Slide jumps into action.

"Your Majesty, I have an additional campaign for you to consider. We know from our research that Direct Mail is not dead. In fact, we know, statistically speaking, that we can expect about a two percent response to our effort. This number excites us because it means we can increase our business opportunity by using Direct Mail correctly. So, we're looking at doing a wave mailing consisting of four oversized color postcards. We're acquiring a targeted list, and we're using a printing company that will personalize the mailing. The same card will go out three times in a row every two weeks. The fourth card is going to look the same, but it's going to have an offer to provide a free no obligation survey of their facility. They will be encouraged to pick up the phone and contact us. What do you think?"

"What good would that do?" said the King.

Slide and Igor are now looking at each other. They can't understand why these marketing promotions are not exciting the King who has been lectur-ing about these in his Master Class series for the last year.

Igor steps forward. "Your Majesty. I have another promotion for you to con-sider."

"Very well. proceed."

"Well, the biggest problem in this economy is developing reasons why a prospect should use our services as opposed to our competition. If one can identify a true competitive advantage, and market it successfully, then we'll be in a position to win more business."

Igor stops waiting for a response from the King. Nothing. So, Igor continues.

"We have identified an author who develops books for construction companies. Ron McKenzie *(shameless self–promotion)* goes into a company and develops a competitive–advantage book that subliminally promotes the firm's attributes and how that firm provides an extraordinary service. Ron publishes the book and it instantly appears online at Amazon and other online bookstores ready to order. It can even be published as a Kindle Book. Also, any bookstore retailer can order it. We get the books for our clients and prospects at the publishers cost. The competition doesn't know how to respond. They are, in fact, stumped. It will take over a year to catch up, and meanwhile, we'll be noticed by many companies, some we know, and some that are new to us. What do you think?"

"What good would that do?" responded the King.

Igor and Slide look at each other. Normally the King would be jumping up and down at these tactical promotions.

Slide steps forward. "Your Majesty, if I may, it seems you're not excited at all about our promotions. Perhaps you could tell us what's missing?"

The King smiles. "When I answered, 'What good would that do?' I was being facetious. Anyone who says that obviously doesn't know the first thing about marketing. The point is, there are managers out there that actually think this way. They are watching their business die, and they are helpless. They have no idea of what to do. There is hope for construction marketing after all. Congratulations to both of you."

An AEC firm cannot do all of the marketing tactics that are available. That is why the marketing plan exists, which carefully looks at the market and their budget, develops the promotions, implements and then measures the success. The longer this is done, the better they are to hit their target market with just the right message.

STORY #53
P.S.

THE KING AND HIS ENTOURAGE were walking in the Market Square enjoying the bright and sunny day. The King was particular happy as his Kingdom was prospering. Buyers and sellers were busy haggling over prices in animated happy voices. Suddenly the King recognized his head architect for the Castle, Slide Rule of Building Blocks, Inc., and Igor, from Moat Designs, Ltd., who was the general contractor for the Castle.

"Greetings on this fine day," said the King. "So, what's going on, if I may ask?"

Slide and Igor immediately rose up to greet the King, while other traders and buyers looked on enviously of the friendly relationship Slide and Igor had with their King.

A chair was immediately made available for the King.

"Good morning your Majesty. We were sitting here reviewing a business letter that Igor is writing. It's an important letter to a prospect introducing his company. Igor would like Moat Designs to be considered in the future to provide construction services for them. It could mean a lot of money to Igor."

"Very good. Igor, may I also look at the letter?"

Igor smiled. "That would be great. You probably get many of these letters, and you might have some helpful hints."

Slide handed the letter to the King, who took it, and read the letter carefully.

The King looks up. "Is this it?"

Igor looks surprised. "Why yes. Is something's missing?"

"Well, to start, you really didn't introduce yourself to the reader, and there's no subject line to tell them what the letter is about. In addition, you don't really tell the reader the benefit of your services. It appears you want their business, but you never really asked for the order. On top of all that, there's no P.S."

"What?"

"So, no P.S. Big deal?"

"Do you know what the P.S. means?"

"No idea your Majesty."

"P.S. is an abbreviation for Postscript, meaning additional information, in this case, at the end of a letter. It can help you make money."

"So?" said Slide.

"It's the most important part of the letter."

"How so?"

"First, let me ask you a question. How does one read a letter?"

Slide and Igor looked at each other and realized that another Master Class was now in session.

Igor and Slide again exchange glances. "It's a trick question," whispered Slide to Igor.

"I heard that," said the King. "I'm going to ignore it for the time being. The way a letter is read is the reader glances at the logo of the company, and their eyes slide down to who it was addressed to, and then glances at the subject line, and then reads the first several words of the first sentence, and then drops immediately down to the signature, and then reads the P.S."

"Really," said Igor.

"Yes, studies have been done on how people read letters, and more often than not, the P.S. is read before the body of the letter is read in its entirety."

"Really? Why?"

"Because it tells the reader the main subject and benefits of the letter very quickly so they can determine how seriously they're going to pay attention to the main body of the letter."

"So, that would mean you actually should put something very important in the P.S."

"Very good Igor."

Igor swells with pride. "So, what kind of ideas should I put into the P.S.?"

"What are you selling?"

"Construction services."

"So, perhaps the P.S. should read . . . PS: Moat Designs have helped many businesses with their construction projects, whether commercial, industrial, or residential, and consistently have shown them ways to save money. We can also discuss about providing a free roof inspection, as well as windows and doors, and exterior block condition, in the form of a life-cycle cost analysis."

"Wow, your Majesty. I'm really impressed," said Igor.

P.S. You're reading this aren't you? See, I knew you would. If you need an experienced construction industry strategic, business and marketing consultant, who can help you develop more business and increase revenue, please send me an email at ramckenzie.compass@gmail.com. Or visit my web site at www.compassconsultantscorp.com. (shameless self–promotion).

211

STORY #54
Asking for the Order

"LOST ANOTHER ONE," said Slide to the King, the undisputed ruler and owner of the Castle.

Slide Rule was the head architect for the Castle and the prestigious owner of Building Blocks, Inc. Sitting next to them was Igor from Moat Designs, Ltd. who was the general contractor of the Castle. They had stopped at the Market Square for a midday meal.

"Seems like you have said that a lot lately," said the King.

"I've been making a lot of presentations, and I'm not getting anywhere."

"Slide, perhaps you can use some help with your presentations?" suggested the King.

"Not me. I have it down to a science. *Get In; Get Out.* That's my motto."

"That's the goal of your presentation?" asked Igor.

"Yes. I dare say you have the same goal when you present."

"It's not true. I operate strictly on a basis of providing the best image of my company."

The King was definitely getting more interested. "So, what do you mean by that, Igor?"

"I use the **Last In; First Out** technique."

The King is getting a bit edgy at Igor who seemed to be avoiding a direct answer. The King took another sip of his watered down wine, and turned toward Igor. "What does that mean?"

"Whoever is the newest staff person in my company automatically makes the presentation. That way they can get experience and ramp up faster."

"Does this technique work," asked Slide.

"No, not at all."

"So why don't you, the owner of your company, who is responsible for sales, be the one who speaks to your new potential clients," asked the King. "It would be a perfect time to develop a relationship with them."

"I'm not going in and speaking in front of people. Are you crazy?"

The King was now very agitated. He got up and started to pace back and forth. He looked at both of them.

"Uh, oh, said Igor. I think another Master Class has started."

"You're both idiots. **Get In; Get Out,** and **Last In; First Out.** You both need help and I'm not sure if it's mental help or marketing help, or both. But, as your King, I'm here to help."

"How can you help us, your Majesty," said Igor.

Suddenly, platters of food arrived at their table. The King waved off the food, which immediately disappeared. Igor and Slide watched the food vanish longingly, since they were both very hungry. It felt like their last meal had just vaporized.

"That will be your last meal if you don't pay attention!"

Igor and Slide looked at each other.

"Igor, how does he read our minds?" whispered Slide.

Igor shrugs his shoulders. "I think it's the author."

The King cleared his throat, and his students immediately give him their full attention.

"The very best way to attract business is to make a confident presentation. First, the prospect, want to see the owners of the company presenting, or for very large company, the people in charge that have the title. It's certainly alright to have others present. But they definitely don't want to see the lowest person in the company giving the presentation, who basically got thrown under the bus to give the presentation."

Igor looks at Slide and shrugs his shoulders.

"Being thrown under the bus is an idiomatic phrase meaning to sacrifice another person. That means you, the owners and principals of your company must make the presentation. So, your **Last In; First Out** idea doesn't work. Next, one sign of confidence is showing up yourself. So your **Get In; Get Out** philosophy is not going to work."

"Realizing the King is probably right, Igor raises his hand. Can you give us a tip that will help us get the order when we're presenting?"

"Yes. Remember this, most architects and contractors at the end of their presentation will turn and walk out of the room, as as they have very little sales training. Some don't even say thank you for being invited. Actually, to them, the ending is a relief. But a good architect and contractor will stand there and make a close. You see, you must sincerely ask for the order, and at the same time interweave everything you have learned about the hot points of the owners into your close. Not doing so is one of the biggest mistakes made in presentations in all industries."

Can you give us an example?"

"Let me summarize for you. I've known both of you for a long time, and we've worked before on different projects. I want to say thank you for allow-ing me to talk about how I can help you you're your presentations. But, I also want to say, I sincerely and respectfully ask for you to allow me to coach you further, on your closing abilities. You'll see, as we've demonstrated here, we make a good team, and a good team means we'll work together on any issue that presents itself. It's not always about the money; it's really about the working relationships we have together as we move forward. There will always be issues, but if the team can address them together, then there really aren't any issues at all. I invite you to visit my office so we can discuss this project together."

"You're hired," Igor and Slide said in unison.

If you want an easy way to beat your competition, and win more contracts, then form a team that becomes an expert in giving sincere presentations that discusses the value of your company while talking about their company, and at the end, you'll always ask for the order. Learn to say thank you, and we would love to work with you and your team.

STORY #55
The Expert

"I'M NOT GOING TO DO IT," announced Slide.

The King, owner of the Castle, stood at the fence rail and offered a handful of hay to a cow. The cow immediately took a liking to the King, and became his best friend.

Slide Rule, owner of Building Blocks, Inc., the chief architect of the Castle stood next to the King, and on the other side of the King stood Igor, who was from Moat Designs, Ltd., the general contractor of the Castle.

After the King finished feeding the cow, they all wandered down the road to the Market Square and decided to stop for lunch at an outside café.

"So Slide, what are you not going to do?" asked the King as they sat down in the shade. Cold brews were immediately served.

"I was asked to give a speech."

"A speech? What a great opportunity!" said the King."

Igor laughs.

The King glares at Igor. "Why are you laughing?"

"I wouldn't do the speech either."

The King took a deep long draw of his afternoon brew, and set his mug down loudly. "Let me tell you a story. An architect, like you Slide, went into consulting after writing a book published by McGraw-Hill, a major publisher. He was invited to speak at a prestigious gathering of contractors, and although reluctant, he decided he would give the speech to launch his consulting career, but only on one condition – his first speech was to be his last, as he didn't want to rely on speaking to get his consulting engagements."

"So what happened." asked Igor.

"Well, he gave the speech, which ran a little over an hour, and at the end there was a question and answer session which went very well. As he left the podium he was very relieved it was over, and also knew it was his first and last speech."

"So, if I may ask your Majesty, how does this help Slide who has already decided not to speak?"

"Well, let me continue the story." The King got up and started to pace. Another Master Class was in session. "The architect stayed for lunch and had several conversations with contractors who asked him even more questions. Then on his way out to his car, his cell phone rang, and he looked and it was an unfamiliar number."

"Cell phone?" questioned Slide.

"A future thing. As it turned out, the call was from a vice-president of a very large sub-contractor based in Chicago. The VP told him he liked what he had to say at the morning presentation, and invited him to their offices for a meeting the following week. The first meeting went well, and after several meetings they became his client. Over the next eight years he worked with them behind the scenes, traveling far-and-wide to multiple states to help other divisions of their company to attract new business."

"Doesn't matter, I'm still not going to stand up in front of people and speak," said Slide. "I have no passion for making speeches. It's a waste of time and all they do is get information from you for free. And besides, who wants to stand up in front of a room and talk. The thought makes me want to throw up."

"Ah, so you have a fear of public speaking."

"I have absolutely no fear of public speaking. There is no way I'm going to do it, so there isn't any fear involved."

Igor shook his head. "I don't know, it's starting to look like a pretty good opportunity to me."

The King stopped pacing and took another long sip of his brew. "The story gets better."

"Really," said Slide.

"The next morning he received another phone call, and it was from a construction management company, and he later met with them and also signed a consulting agreement. That relationship lasted for over five years."

"Really," said Slide again.

"So, what happened?" asked Igor.

"Despite his vow never to speak again, he became a regular speaker at conventions, seminars, peer groups as well as universities. He learned that the secret to speaking is being over-prepared, and having an absolutely great and powerful PowerPoint slide presentation. He also learned to make the close."

"What's the close?"

The King smiled. "The speaker will make some kind of offer to do business together. He asks for the order in a very subliminal way."

Slide has been very quiet.

"So, Slide. What's your decision?"

"I've decided to throw my hat into the ring. But I've one question. What is your goal as a speaker?"

The King sat back down at the table. "Like the cow that ate the hay from my hand, a good speaker will have the audience eating out of their hand, because when you speak, you're considered an expert in your field."

The story of the speech and the two clients is a true story, and the author is still speaking to this day helping contractors grow their business. If you're a principal of a firm and get the opportunity to make a speech, even if it's on a panel, then do it.

STORY #56
Web Site or Just a Sign?

SLIDE RULE'S NEW WIDE FORMAT SIGN was hanging on the side of the Castle's rock wall overlooking the Market Square.

Slide Rule, of Building Blocks, Inc., the architect of record for the Castle, and Igor, the King's favorite builder and owner of Moat Designs, Ltd., stood on either side of the King, looking up at the sign.

"So, Igor, what do you think of Slide's new sign located on my Castle wall?" the King asked.

"I'm duly impressed," said Igor. "Good location for all traders and buyers to see."

"How about you Slide?"

Slide was becoming a bit worried. "Your Majesty, I thought I would put up the sign to try and get some business. I should have asked for your permission."

"Oh, don't worry Slide, I'm not mad that you used the Castle wall to promote yourself without asking me. I just wanted to talk about the sign."

Slide breathed a sigh of relief. "Do you have any comments about my sign?" your Majesty.

"Actually, yes. I think you could have improved your company's message."

"How so?"
"Well, you're not identified as the lead architect, and primary contact."

"Good point. I should have put that on there."

"Also, there's no real explanation of the services you offer."
"You're right again. I should've thought of that."

Igor had been listening to the conversation. "Slide, how long do you expect this to be up here?"

"I was thinking around two-to-three years."

"Really?" said the astonished King, looking at Slide.

"What's wrong with that?"

"Well, the problem is you're making the same mistake that the majority of companies make regarding their business web site."

"Web site?"

"You know. That future electronic thing where people can see what you're all about."

"What kind of mistake?"

"Well, many companies complete their web site, and then it sits there for years as if nothing was happening in their business. Just like your sign."

"So, are you saying that these future web sites need to be updated on a regular basis?"

"Yes, exactly. But there's more. Most web sites are like your rather boring sign, they don't provide any value. Give someone who sees your sign a reason to contact you."

"That's very interesting. I never thought of that."

The King continued. "Make it a place where people come back to get information. For example, list the speaking engagements of the principals as well as other executives in your business. That's very impressive to the target market. Also, provide copies of articles the principals have written for construction trade magazines. You might even tease them with a brief excerpt from a book the marketing principal is writing. Feature new press releases. There are so many things that can be done."

"Are you saying I should do the same thing with my sign?"

"Yes, but in a different way. Signs get old. If you replaced the content, and kept you logo, you would have a fresh looking sign, and start to establish a brand at the same time. Prospects would start to identify you with the services you provide. Most businesses just put up some flashy graphics and then leave it there forever. Signs should talk to the reader."

"Like the web sites you keep talking about?"

"Yes, exactly. Most construction web sites are just like a sign."

"Do you have anymore examples of value that should be communicated?"

"Simple. Demonstrate your company's unique value. Show them that you can help them solve their problem; that you can save them money, because you care and have expertise that other's don't have. Be up-to-date with technology. For example, a slow loading web site will make prospects go look for your competitor."

"So, while a sign is a static communication device, a web site is meant to constantly change and provide reasons to come back to it. To communicate, if you will."

"Yes. Perfect. So, what do you call a web site that's like a sign?"

"A cobweb," answered Slide.

A web site is not a business card.

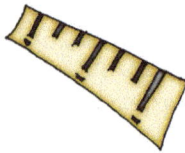

STORY #57
The Envelope Please

"DIRECT MAIL IS FOR THE BIRDS," said Igor, owner of Moat Designs, Ltd. "What did you say?" asked the King.

"I meant to say that using direct mail as a source to generate leads, that in turn, lead to profitable assignments, is not really a good business investment."

"That's what I thought you said."

"I'm sorry, your Majesty, but I just spent a fortune on a mailing, and the results were dreadful."

"Perhaps it was how your mailing looked when they received it," said Slide Rule the owner of Building Blocks, Inc. the general contractor for the Castle.

"What would you know about that?" said Igor.

"Actually, I hate to admit it, but Slide has a good point," replied the King. Slide beamed in all his glory.

"It's time for lunch, and another Master Class. I invite both of you to sit with me and we'll discuss some important factors regarding direct mail marketing. It could very well make you a rich beyond your wildest dreams."

"You're serious," responded Slide.

"Yes, why do you ask?"

"I never thought of you as being an expert in anything," answered Slide.

"Really!"

"Slide, if I were you I would rephrase that last statement. That's one of those off with your head kind of remarks that could get you in trouble with the King. Your Majesty, I barely know Slide, and I consider you an expert in all things."

"Your Majesty, I in no way intended to slight you in any way. My very good and close friend Igor would attest to that."

Igor took one step away from Slide.

"Both of you are acting like village idiots. Sit here with me at this new Market Square restaurant. Let us eat and talk."

They all sat down and King ordered for everyone, and watered down wine was promptly served.

"So, let me make this very clear, direct mail marketing works. Even in the future when there are other alternatives for companies getting their message in front of prospects, such as social media and web sites. Direct mail is a viable marketing tool."

"But my mailing failed miserably," said Igor.

"Let me see what it looks like?"

Igor pulled out of his bag several unopened mail pieces and handed them to the King and to Slide.

The King examines them as their order of chips and dip arrived. "This is one of the most unimpressive, impassionate pieces of mail I have ever seen. Why should I open this?"

"I couldn't answer that," said Slide. I also got one in the mail, and I never opened it either."

"Okay, first of all, there are several types of direct mail consisting of various kinds of offers. There is also a direct mail program referred to as a wave mailing that works rather well. A wave mailing is a series of direct mail pieces building up to an offer."

Igor promptly waves his hand to everyone in the room. "Done, he exclaims. Hardly cost a thing."

The King looks at Igor as Slide slowly inches his chair away from him.

Igor suddenly realizes there must be another form of wave mailing and he immediately becomes quiet and attentive. "Sorry, your Majesty."

The King continues, shaking his head at Igor. "No matter what kind of mailing that's done it must be an attractive piece in order for them to either open the envelope or to read the postcard The message must pique their curiosity."

"Are you saying this mailing is unattractive?" asked Igor.

"Your Majesty, may I take the lead on this?" said Slide.

"Yes, by all means."

"Igor, your mailing is U-G-G-L-L-L-Y!"

"Ugly. How can you say that?"

"He's right" said the King. "It's one of the most unattractive envelopes I've ever seen. To make a point, you're familiar with the Academy Awards, aren't you?"

"Yes. Sure. Everyone is familiar with Academy Awards and the Oscar."

"Well, the presenter always walks out carrying an envelope. One presenter at the awards, Tom Hanks, made the comment that the envelope was the most beautifully designed one he had ever seen, and it was a work of art. He was making a point that can be translated back to direct mail marketing. The mailing piece must be well designed in order for it to be opened, and the message must be clear and entertaining. In fact, the reader starts to gain interest in the product or service as the direct mail is solving a problem or satisfying a need. Most direct mail pieces don't do this, in fact, most direct mail pieces in envelopes never get opened. It's why most direct mail campaigns fail."

"I had no idea. I never thought of direct mail in those terms."

"So, what's your response?"

"The envelope, please."

Direct mail is a design problem. For a good mailing the industry standard response you should expect is around 2%. Also remember, direct mail is only one marketing tactic to get your message in front of your target market, but it is a trusted and tested form of marketing.

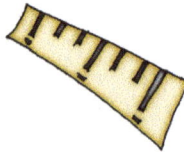

STORY #58
Going Green

THE KING PACED BACK AND FORTH as Igor, the owner of Moat Designs, Ltd., and Slide Rule, of Building Blocks, Inc., the King's No. 1 architect sat before him.

"If good design is now considered GREEN design, why are so many not doing it?"

Igor and Slide Rule looked at each other knowing they were in for a long Master Class.

The King continued to pontificate. "This is an important question as it's quite certain that GREEN design and construction practices are not going to disappear anytime soon. Is GREEN design relevant? Consider the fact that it adds a complexity to the construction process as well as increase the cost."

Igor and Slide Rule sat there helplessly unable to answer the King.

The King continued. "GREEN costs money and now feeds a multi-million dollar industry. In some cases LEED certified projects are simply verifying that the subject building without any changes meets a certain LEED criteria. So, what's the rush? Why go through the process at all?"

"Perhaps they do not really understand the true importance of the meaning of sustainability," suggested Igor proudly. Slide Rule gave him a dirty look and shook his head.

"I totally agree, but I, the King, believe the answer is in the way LEED benefits are perceived. For example, if I were to take a paper shilling and ask you if you want it, would you take it?

"I would," said Igor.

"Add me to the list," said Slide Rule.

"So, if I crumple it up, would you still want it?" The King crumpled up the bill. "Works for me," said Igor.

Slide Rule gave Igor a look of worry. Was the moat contractor going to get the paper shilling, or was he, the architect, going to get the money?

The King drops the money on the floor and stamps on it. "How about now?"

"It's a keeper," said Slide who felt he had to participate more in these conversations to get on the good side of the King.

"Why do you want this dirty crumpled shilling? It's in terrible shape."

"Because, it's still worth a shilling," exclaimed Slide Rule.

"Right," said the King. "Right! It's still worth a shilling. By comparison, if you really haven't gone through the process of sustainability in a formal manner, then there is a loss of VALUE. Just because you said the building meets certain criteria, doesn't mean it is. The value of the LEED certification process is that you are using the process."

Igor and Slide Rule nodded in agreement. Or was it bewilderment?

"If I were to ask each one of you to rate yourself between one and ten, how would you do so?"

"I, for myself, knowing what I do, and how I do it, would rate myself high," said Slide in a triumph manner. "An 8 or a 9."

"How would you rate Igor, Slide?"

"He would get about a 6 out of a 10."

"What?" exclaimed Igor.

"Hey, the moat still leaks. What can I say?"

"See, that's my point. If we rate ourselves, we're going to rate ourselves high, and this is backed up by studies. But, it we let an independent body rate ourselves, like the LEED program does, then we can be assured that we are going to get a fair independent rating. That's the value of the LEED program. People and companies think they are providing the same level of sustainability, but in reality, if they don't go through the process, they'll never really know."

"Okay, whatever you say," said Slide Rule eager to get the meeting over.

Igor thought for a moment. "So what you really mean is that if a tree falls in the woods, it doesn't make a sound unless we are there to hear it."

The King and Slide Rule looked at Igor in a strange way.

GREEN is important for our planet. It's even more important for the AEC community as it communicates we are up-to-date in our profession, and interested in conservation. It is the author's opinion that LEED criteria will eventually become interweaved into the various building codes. LEED will continue to exist, but it means that companies will still need to budget for LEED to meet the requirements of the building code.

STORY #59
The Treasure

A LONG LINE OF TRAVELERS followed the King down the winding path as they moved away from the Castle. A large group of Knights in Shining Armor traveled in front of the King for protection.

"This is a great day. I'm happy and ready for anything. How about you Slide Rule?" asked the King.

"Well, the truth is, your Majesty, while I'm excited about treasure hunting, I'm not happy. It seems like this is a lot of work and inconvenience to seek out this fortune."

"I agree with Slide," said Igor, who was the general contractor for the Castle and owner of Moat Designs, Ltd.

"Slide, as the chief architect for the Castle, I thought you would enjoy a day away from your prospering business of architecture. Building Blocks, Inc. is the leading architect of this region. You should be really happy."

"Well, your Majesty. I'm not happy. Everyday it's something else that needs my attention. Nothing seems to go right. It's an endless stream of frustrations."

"And, you Igor. What are your worries and frustrations that cause you to be unhappy as the manager of your business?"

"To be honest. Everything. It's hard to be happy when a meteor is headed for the earth and we're all doomed."

Slide is looking up in the sky. "You're kidding. Now I have to worry about that too!"

The King is smiling and laughing and having a wonderful day. "It's an expression you idiot."

"We told you our problems and you're making fun of us. Why? How can you say that?" asked Slide. "Is your happiness at our expense?"

"Oh, it's really not all that bad. Listen, what if I revealed to you the secret to happiness in business and in life. You as business owners and managers of people could use this information to help those around you and then they too will become more productive, and being more productive means being more profitable."

Slide pondered this statement. "Does it mean I'll have to do something? I've got enough to do."

"Yes, by all means. Being happy is hard work as it means you will have to change how you think. I'm going to tell you the secret of happiness. But you must promise me you'll use it and also impart it to others that are in your employ. What do you say?"

"It sounds good to me," replied Igor. Slide nods his head in agreement.

"Okay, here's the answer. You must choose to be happy now."

Igor looks at the sky. "Where is that meteor when we need it?"

"I'm with you," said Slide also looking up in the sky.

"I'm serious. That's the answer," responded the King.

"Come on. You just sold us down the river on that one. You got us good." said Igor.

"Okay. Now listen to this. There's nothing stopping you from being happy right now. Of course everyone has life challenges, but even those challenges are not enough to keep you from just being happy. Choose to be happy and all kinds of wonderful things start to happen. First, your body chemistry changes and you will feel better. Next, people will want to be around you and learn from you. Being happy and having a positive demeanor will help you move in the direction that you want to go and to get the things you want

231

in your life. People will want to help you. If your staff took this attitude you would find that problems will be solved faster as you would eliminate the adversarial relationships."

"You really believe that?" asked Igor.

The King turned around and gave Igor a very forlorn look which caused him to shrink backwards and try to hide. Then the King broke into a big smile and laughter. "Of course I do. You must choose to be happy and it will change you."

"I never doubted you for a moment," said Igor.

Slide was laughing. "I'm getting happier by the minute. Do you think that being happy will help us find the buried treasure?"

"Oh, I know where the treasure is buried. I've known for years. I just wanted to be out and enjoy the day. You see, if you're happy, you don't really need the treasure and everything you'll need will come to you."

"You know where the treasure is buried? said Slide rather astounded at the news.

"Yes. Always have," replied the King.

"So that means we're not going to find it today?" Igor asked a bit disappointed.

"Yup, said the King.

"Maybe you're happy because you know where the treasure is buried?

"Perhaps you and Slide should be happy because you know someone who knows where the treasure is buried?

"Works for me," said Igor.

"This happiness thing is going to be great," said Slide.

Maybe being happy is the real treasure.

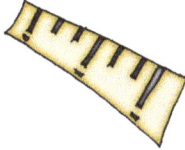

STORY #60
Etiquette and All the King's Men

THE KING WAS MAD. He paced back and forth in the main chamber of the glorious Cathedral that was completely empty. He was so mad, his Knights in Shinning Armor that guarded him were afraid to enter, and as a consequence, hung around the exterior doors hoping they wouldn't be called upon. Beside the King was a small table with three empty mugs.

Slide Rule, the King's No. 1 architect came running passed the guards and into the room. The Knights knew him and let him pass thankful there was someone for their King to talk too.

"Your Majesty. I'm sorry I'm late," said Slide totally out of breath.

"You don't look sorry," answered the King. "You look late."

Oh, oh, thought Slide. "Your Majesty. It couldn't be helped. I found out last night I had to go to a construction site."

Slide looks around the room. "Hey, where's Igor?"

"You tell me," answered the King who continued to pace briskly back-and-forth.

"You mean you've been here alone? I thought Igor would be here."

"You thought?"

Slide knew immediately things were not going well.

Just then Igor, the King's award winning moat contractor arrives also out of breath. "I'm sorry I'm late. Thank you Slide for covering for me."

"Slide just got here," announced the King.

Igor glances at Slide, and then the King. "Oh, oh. I thought Slide was going to be here."

"You thought? . . . Apparently everyone talked to no one and more important, no one talked to me," said the King.

Igor and Slide Rule stood very still in front their King. The Knights were laughing and taking quick peeks into the room thankful it wasn't them.

The King shot the Knights a look and they very quickly became quiet. The King then proceeded to pour himself, Slide and Igor a brew.

"Have a seat," said the King sweeping the room with his arm indicating the bench in front of him. "Or should I say, SIT DOWN?"

Igor and Slide slid on to the bench and were quiet as a church mouse.

Igor take s a sip of his brew. "Hey, this is warm."

"Well, it was cold when I GOT HERE," said the King.

Igor and Slide looked at each other, and shrunk down even lower on their bench.

"So, I arrived here early to enjoy your company and to discuss the business of the Cathedral and both of you were not here. Why is it that no one informed me?"

"I figured that Slide was going to be here. So I figured it was okay," answered Igor.

"You figured….?"

"Figure of speech."

"Lot's of figuring going on here," said the King in his best sarcastic voice.

"So, I take it from the conversations, and also from your figuring, that both of you knew last night but neither one of you communicated to me, the King, and in fact, even with each other. Is that correct?"

"Yes," Igor and Slide said in unison.

The King turned away from them for a second and Slide hit Igor in the arm.

"Enough of that Slide," said the King.

Igor is rubbing his sore arm wondering how the King knew Slide hit him. Must be that 'all knowing King stuff,' he thought.

"Have either one of you ever heard of business etiquette?"

"Is that where you're supposed to be polite to your fellow worker and also to those you engage to do work for you?" asked Slide.

"Yes, but it's more then that. It's about being courteous and thoughtful to the people around you. It's about apologizing when you step on some one's toes. It's about presenting yourself at business meetings with good manners and making guest feel comfortable. It's about keeping your business associates, like the King, informed of your schedule if there is a change. It's about not becoming pushy with a new prospect so that they're uncomfortable; it's about making the right toast at a gathering," said the King.

"Your Majesty. You have made a great speech and both Slide and I are humbled in your presence. I would like to make a toast."

They all pick up a mug of brew.

"To our all knowing King, who makes us better-and-better."

"Figures," says the King.

Say a person, which we'll name Rude, is rude to some one from another company, which we'll call Memory. When Rude is rude, Memory not only remembers the rude person, but remembers the company Rude works for, and based upon that, makes a conclusion that they may not want to do business with that company. You are remembered by how you present yourself to others.

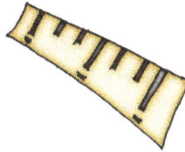

STORY #61
A Better View

"**LET'S TALK ABOUT THE FUTURE,**" said the King to Slide and Igor. This knoll looks like a good place to stop."

The King headed over toward a grassy knoll and his servants raced ahead of them to put down some large pieces of heavy cloth to make their King more comfortable.

"This is the life," the King stated.

Igor, of Moat Designs, Ltd. and Slide Rule of Building Blocks, Inc., the Kings No. 1 architect joined the King on the grassy knoll.

"I like this spot. It has a nice picket fence and we can view the road that comes from the left and goes downhill and away from us. We can see everything from here."

Igor and Slide agreed with the King and settled back to enjoy the rest and conversation.

"So Igor, how are you going to change your marketing this year?" asked the King.

"I'm not. Same story, new date."

"How about you, Slide? Are you making any changes?"

"Nope. Marketing is an expense. I'm not going to change anything. In fact, I may cut it down a bit."

"Big mistake," said the King.

Igor was rather surprised and somewhat upset. "But your Majesty, we cannot change. It's too expensive to change, and besides, what's the point? There's a structural economic recession going on throughout the Kingdom."

The all knowing King smiled. "But you're missing a huge opportunity because you still need to surround your prospects with your marketing message.

Especially now, because when the market comes back they will remember you."

"I don't understand." replied Slide. Igor agreed.

The King waved his hand and watered down wine was immediately served. Another Master Class had started. "Let me explain it to you. Understand, everything in life changes. Everything!"

"Everything?" questioned Igor.

"Yup. Let me give you an example. Doctors, lawyers, teachers and preachers were once respected members of our community. Now, doctors live in fear of lawyers who live well off the doctors. Preachers preach about what is being taught in schools while the teachers are not allowed to mention churches."

"I'm so confused," said Igor.

"Well, let me put it this way. Marketing is an ever changing sea of dreams."

"That's good, said Slide. "You should write a book on marketing."

"Thank you Slide. I'll tell that to the author. Anyway, what I mean is that 'needs and wants' of your target market changes. You must keep your marketing message current reflecting your marketing intelligence of the current trends. This also means you might be considering different delivery options."
"How so?" questioned Igor.

"Well, think of it this way. Exercise coaches say that you should vary your workout, because if you do the same thing over-and-over again, your body responds and it becomes easy, also meaning your workouts become easy. These coaches say you should vary your exercise routine so you are hitting different muscles at different times, or hitting different muscles in a different ways. The result is you become better fit."

Slide flexes his arm and looks at his bicep. The King ignores him.

Igor, who had been paying attention, asks, "So what you're saying, is we need to vary our marketing to our prospects so they don't become complacent, which means after awhile they'll start to ignore our message."

"Very good Igor," stated the King.

"So instead of using electronic mail, I might actually use a postcard mailing. That will really surprise them."

"Perfect. And because there's always change we need to hit them from different angles but also with different messages. And that's because we're keeping track of what their needs and wants are, which allows us to market to them."

The King is getting excited that his marketing message is getting through. "Here's another point. You never know which marketing tactic is going to work. If you did know you could become very wealthy very fast."

"So, what do we do?" asked Igor.

"You must do two things, test your tactics and use a variety of marketing solutions, not just one over-and-over."

Slide is now interested. "So you want us to keep track, say like a scorecard, to measure the response of what works and what doesn't work. Is that it?"

"Yes, yes," replied the King. You've got it."

Everything changes and you need to market as many ways as you can, because you don't know which one of them is going to make a difference. Look at marketing from different views and apply what you learn.

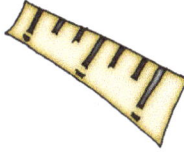

STORY #62
Lost Order Means a Step Forward

SLIDE RULE TAKES OFF HIS HAT IN DISGUST, and then bows respectively toward the King. Slide was the owner of Building Blocks, Inc. and the head architect for the Castle.

"My, you are apparently upset about something," said the King.

The contractor for the Castle, Igor of Moat Designs, who already had an audience with the King, laughs at Slide's plight. "Oh, he just lost a big commission. I told him to move on to the next one."

"You told him to move on. Is that your advice Igor?"

"Yup. He's not going to get any business from that guy. As they say, fuggedaboudit."

"Tell me more about it."

"Well, I was called for an interview about two years ago. We were short listed, so we made the presentation but were not selected. The owner said to me in confidence he really wanted to use my services, but his Board of Directors decided otherwise."

"They always say that," said Igor. They're just trying to make you feel better."

"Let Slide continue," said the King. "And, in the spirit of the occasion, a round of wine for everyone. Slide, please tell us more."

"Well, about a year passes by, and I got a call as they had a problem with a parapet rock wall. They couldn't make it work, so they asked me to come down and take a look. I did an investigation and found where the problem was, and suggested ways to fix it. They thanked me, and then I never heard anything from them."

"So, you recently got a call again?"

"Yes. They wanted to interview several architects, so I went down and made a presentation, and, if I do say so myself, it went very well. But the results were the same. I was not selected."

"Lose the guy," said Igor.

"Did he say anything to you like last time?"

"Well, I got a message this morning. The message said they really appreciated my effort, and they were very close to making a switch, but decided not to do it. He said, sooner or later we'll work together."

Igor threw his hands up in the air. "Same story. I'm telling you they all say that. He's just trying to get free work from you."

"Well, taking everything into consideration, you are one step closer to getting a deal with him," said the King.

"Being one step closer doesn't pay the salaries around here," commented Slide as he downed his wine.

"But you're wrong. Very wrong indeed."

"How is that your Majesty?"

"The missed sales of yesterday are the sales that are paying your crew today."

Igor scratched his head. "Let me think about that. You're saying it's OK to have a missed sale?"

"Yes. Certainly. Sales, particularly product and service sales are a relationship business. Now, it might seem that having all of these interactions is leading you away from the deal. But the opposite is true; you're getting closer-and-closer. Did you send a thank you note to your prospect?"

"Why waste the paper," said Igor.

"The King turned and looked at Igor. "Let me remind you that when your buddy here gets an architectural commission it generally leads to construction. That's potential work for you."

"Oh."

There was a pause as everyone was thinking.

"Say Slide," says Igor. How about that note?"

"What about it?"

Igor continues. "Let's do this. Write out the note and then let's you and I make a visit together. You can personally hand him the note, and you can introduce me. I'll bring a little present, like a fine bottle of wine."

"Perfect," said the King. "Keep on servicing your clients and prospects, and when business is slow, over service them. And I'll do my part, I'll provide the bottle of wine from own wine cellar, and you can tell him for me that the King appreciates his business in my area, and look forward to meeting him."

"It can't get any better then that," said Slide. "Cheers."

Some companies become clients quickly; some take
a long time to sign. But when they do, they are
generally worth the effort.

STORY #63
Live From New York

"IT'S SATURDAY NIGHT," said the King. "So, where's everyone going this evening?" The King sat down in a shaded area near to the entrance of his Castle.

Slide Rule, of Building Blocks, Inc., the architect of record for the Castle, glances at Igor, the King's favorite builder, and owner of Moat Designs, Ltd. They both rise to acknowledge the King's presence.

Slide took the bait. "Well, your Majesty. Slide and I are taking a short break and then we're going back to work. In fact, we're going to work most of the night, plus all day tomorrow."

"What's the rush?"

"Actually, it's the new tower remodel you've asked for," responded Slide.

"When we made our inspection, we found the rock walls are failing, and in fact, it's a dangerous situation."

"You could say, we're taking care of business," interrupted Igor. "Your business," he added sarcastically.

Both Slide and the King looked at Igor. Slide took one giant step to the left, distancing himself from Igor, who now realized he had made a mistake as to how he had addressed the King.

"I'm greatly offended by your statement Igor. I've been good to you and Slide. You both need a rest, so I hereby fire you both, effective immediately. Also, let me remind you, it's my opinion that by working so much, you're not taking care of business at all. In fact, you're neglecting your business and my business. I don't want someone tired working on my Castle."

The King 🏰 McKenzie

"We're fired?" questioned. Slide, who was shocked. He gave Igor a look that wasn't friendly.

Igor bravely took a step forward. "Your Majesty, I profusely apologize for my remark."

The King shrugged his indifference. "It is done."

"Could you explain your thinking for us so we understand why we're fired?" said Igor. "Both Slide and I are very tired taking care of the Castle."

"Yes, I'll help you understand. First, didn't the both of you work last weekend?"

"Yes, your Majesty."

"And the weekend before that?"

"Yes, your Majesty."

"See, that's the point. All work and no play. You know what Albert Einstein said about that, don't you?"

"I don't even know who Albert Einstein is?" commented Igor.

"Albert Einstein was a German-born mathematician who developed the Theory of Relativity."

"I was terrible in math," said Igor.

Einstein once said, '"Do not worry about your difficulties in Mathematics. I can assure you mine are still greater."'

Slide and Igor looked at each other.

"So," the King continued. "Einstein said about work and no play, 'If A is success in life, then A equals X plus Y plus Z.'"

246

"Can you break that down for us," Slide said.

"Certainly. X equals work and is what you love to do, that challenges you and makes you happy to see a job done well. Y is for play, something you enjoy and look forward to. There must be a good balance between work and play."

"What about Z," Igor asked.

"Z is the third part of the equation. Einstein says Z equals keep your mouth shut."

"Oh, oh," said Igor. "That sort of applies to me."

"Yes. Oh, oh is right. You see, the formula for success per Albert Einstein includes something that people often miss. You must be kind to other people. You must respect them no matter if they're your employee, a waiter in a restaurant, a servant at the food market, or a King like me. You must be polite and accommodating and have a good attitude toward others. You don't know when it's your turn to be out in the street. Sort of like you two."

"Oh, Oh," said Igor.

"Yes, it looks like we're back to, uh, oh."

Your Majesty. I again apologize for my behavior. I was tired with all the work we've been doing. I understand now that we must balance work and play, and also, we must have a good attitude."

"Very well. I can see that you're speaking from your heart. I hereby declare that you're now both back to full time status as the King's architect and contractor."

"Thank you, your Majesty," said Igor and Slide.

"One last question," the King said. "What should we do now? What have you learned?"

Slide and Igor looked at each other, and said in unison, "Live from New York It's Saturday night!"

And they all enjoyed themselves knowing the work would be there for them on Monday, and they would be rested, and ready to go. They would also have a good attitude.

**_Sometimes the best thing you can do for yourself
and your business is to rest._**

STORY #64
Secret's in the Sauce

THE KING AND HIS ENTOURAGE were traveling together on a dusty hot road. The King, in all his wisdom, was giving a Master Class lecture to his two compatriots on marketing.

"Okay. This is what we're going to do. We're going to skip lunch and keep on headed for the Castle. That way I can finish my marketing lecture, and then when we get there we can enjoy the evening." said the King.

"Skip lunch?" said Slide Rule of Building Blocks, Inc, the King's No. 1 architect. "It's not that that we need it," replied the King, laughing with great gusto.

"If I may interject," Igor said. "It's a fundamental fact that eating on a regular basis is the key to longevity and good health. I myself eat at least four meals a day. It's a good thing."

The King laughed. "You may be the contractor for the Castle and owner of Moat Designs, Ltd., but you know nothing about food or marketing."

Slide and Igor exchanged glances knowing that it was going to be a long hot afternoon on the road back to the Castle. The King's Knights in Shining Armor followed with two Knights riding point for the King's protection. There was nothing to do but plod onward. And they did, and the dust sprang upward to greet them, and the sweat poured from their brows. It was truly a hot, miserable and hungry day.

"Now, the first thing I want to talk about is the proper way to make barbeque ribs."

"This is not a good time to talk about food," commented Igor.

The King gave a wave of his hand. "Nonsense. The first step, as we all know, is the selection of the right ribs. Figure three-to-four slabs of pork spareribs should do it. Then they must be marinated for at least a day with a special barbeque rub that is a secret only known to me and my head chef. But I'll share it with you. Then the smoking and glazing starts."

"First the rub. This might include, 3 tablespoons Kosher salt, 2 tablespoons Hungarian paprika, 1-1/2 tablespoons ground cumin, 1 tablespoon ground Mediterranean oregano, 2 teaspoons onion powder, 1 teaspoon garlic powder, 1 teaspoon freshly ground black pepper, 1/2 teaspoon allspice, 1/2 teaspoon ground cinnamon. Combine in a small bowl."

"Wow," Slide and Igor said in unison and in agony.

"Rub seasoning mix onto ribs, pressing into surface. Place ribs in jumbo re-sealable plastic bag. Close bag and marinate in the ice chest for at least one day."

"Your Majesty, do you really think it is good to continue on this hot day without stopping for a bite to eat?"

"Nonsense. Let me continue. Then you have to make the barbeque sauce, which includes, 1/2 cup chopped celery, 3 tablespoons chopped onion, 2 tablespoons butter, 1 cup ketchup, 1/4 cup lemon juice, 2 tablespoons brown sugar, 2 tablespoons vinegar, 1 tablespoon Worcestershire sauce, 1 teaspoon dry mustard, and a dash of pepper. I like to throw in some extra brown sugar as it makes a great glaze, thickens up the sauce, and sweetens everything up a bit. It improves 'the bark' or the crust."

"I'm so hungry your Majesty," said Igor.

The King continued enjoying the discussion about ribs. "Place ribs in center of cooking grate using the lowest heat. Grill 1 to 1-1/2 hours or until tender. You might want to close the lid to pick up some of that good old fashioned smoke house taste. Kind of makes you hungry, doesn't it?"

"I'm so hungry I could faint," said Slide.

The King 👑 McKenzie

Just remember what I always say, "The Secret's in the Sauce."

"Nonsense. Five more miles and we'll be home."

Slide is in total misery. "Your Majesty. Could we not stop for a quick rest so that we may eat or drink something? You are making me so hungry I can almost taste those ribs."

Igor speaks up. "Your Majesty. If I may interject, isn't this a column about marketing? You're giving us a recipe for baby back ribs. Really good ribs I might add. They are so good I can almost taste them. You're killing me over here."

"Me too," responded Igor. "All that I can think about is those ribs. In fact, that's the only thing that I'm going to eat tonight."

"Well, this is a column about marketing, and I just gave you a valuable marketing lesson."

"And what is that?" asked Slide.

"Your marketing program, and the tactics you develop, should be just like the recipe I gave you. You can smell the smoke and taste the sauce as it dripped off of those ribs that were perfectly cooked. Likewise, your marketing program must offer the features and benefits of your services in such a way that your prospect can visualize the end result. They quickly see how their needs and wants are addressed. When you learn how to do that, you'll have as much business as you want. All they should be able to think about is your services."

"Oh, said Slide, thinking about what the King had said.

An advance team of Knights could be seen in the distance. They arrived shortly to escort the King to the Castle. With them they brought cold beer, which was poured for the King and his two guests.

They traveled onward, quite happy with their new insights about their business. All was well as they approached the Castle with visions of marketing, or should I say, visions of slabs of pork spare ribs smothered in a special rub with thick barbeque sauce dripping off them, smoked to perfection.

Add zest to your marketing.

Note: "secret's in the sauce" comes from a line said by Sipsey, who was portrayed by Cicily Tyson in the 1991 movie *Fried Green Tomatoes*.

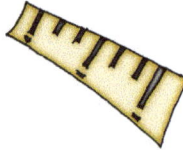

STORY #65
The Lemonade Stand

"**MARKETING!** That`s the answer exclaimed the King. "It's always the answer." Slide rolled his eyes while Igor looked up at the ceiling of the barn.

"Isn't this incredible?" the King said, as he gestured to the magnificent space above them.

Igor, of Moat Designs, Ltd. and Slide Rule of Building Blocks, Inc., the King's No. 1 architect failed to see the point. "So, it's a barn," ventured Igor.

Slide nodded his head in agreement.

"It's not a barn. Don't you know the first thing about marketing?"

"It's a barn," repeated Slide.

The King was now completely energized. "It's not just a barn."

"Then what is it?" asked Slide with less confidence than before.

"It's a marketing opportunity. Don't you see it?"

"No. It's a barn to me. And I think it's a barn to Igor. Right Igor?"

Igor nodded his head in agreement.

The King now started to pace; a sure sign of a Master Class was starting. "Did I ever tell you about selling lemonade when I was a kid?"

"No," responded Igor.

"Well, I sold lemonade at the measly price of five shillings while across the road my competition was selling his for one shilling."

The King ♟ McKenzie

"You must have lost your shirt," stated Slide.

"Quite to the contrary. I made a bloody fortune."

"How did you do that? He had you on price. Who's going to pay four more shillings for the same thing?"

"Before I answer that, I would first like to answer the question about this barn. See, it's not just a barn. It provides shelter for workers that are in transit, and need a place of comfort from the storms. It has sweet smelling hay for the animals and a soft pillow for a night's rest. It's a place to brush your horse, mend a bridle, and a place just to sit and talk with your very best friends."

"Is that what you see?" asked Slide looking around. "I don't see any of that."

"But there's more. The barn provides a comfortable home for cats that in turn eliminate unwanted rodents who also seek out the barn for shelter. There's nothing better then a good barn cat. It also provides a place for owls to perch high above everything so they can see the fields that they prey on. The benefits are endless."

"Okay, so there are a couple of benefits. But that's about all there is?" said Igor.

"Oh no, there's a lot more. It provides a place to store your belongings when you can't find room for them in your Castle. You can also store all of your garden tools so your Castle can look beautiful in the spring, summer and fall."

"Hadn't thought of that," said Slide.

"There's even more. You can have a barn raising which is a great social event and a wonderful charity for a needy neighbor. It strengthens relationships and bonds between people. After that, you can have a barn dance."

"I need to start drinking what you drink," said Slide. "I never saw any of that

254

before."

"See, it's what you market. It's always about marketing. It's always about making yourself different from the competition."

"How about that lemonade? How did you pull that one off?" asked Igor.

"Aha yes. It was nothing more than presentation. I sold my lemonade wearing a tuxedo."

"A tuxedo," said Igor and Slide in unison.

"Yes. A tuxedo. When poor travelers, who were hot and weary from their journey, came down the road and they saw two vendors. One, yours truly, stood there in a full tux with tails balancing two cold crystal glasses on a silver platter delicately on my fingertips, like a maître d' of a fine French restaurant. It was a hot, sultry, humid miserable day, and I appeared cool and confident offering them the same. Across the dusty road was my competition wearing ragged shorts. His table was a mess with dirty glasses and a half picture of lemonade with no ice. When the weary travelers compared the two offerings, they always stopped at mine. See, it was marketing my brand that made the difference. I made a better presentation because I offered them a solution of being their servant and cooling them down from their weary journey. For a few minutes they were the King and I was their humble servant."

"You ought to be in sales, your Majesty," exclaimed Igor.

"I am in sales," assured the King with a big smile.

Think of the needs and wants of your prospect. You must market solutions to those needs and wants to your prospect so they never forget you. It doesn't do any good to market a service you do well if your prospect doesn't need it.

STORY #66
Something's Following You

THE KING TOOK NOTICE OF SLIDE RULE'S DEMEANOR as the King's No. 1 architect and Owner of Building Blocks, Inc. walks into the room and slumps down on a three legged stool.

"So, if I may ask," said the King, "What is going on that gives you such a dismal entrance?" The King takes a sip of his watered down wine.

Just then Igor, of Moat Designs, the contractor for the Castle makes his entrance in a very casual manner, and also slumps down on a stool and leans against the table supporting his head in his hands.

"You too?" stated the King. "Now tell me, it can't be that bad. What's wrong?"

Igor looks at the King and then at Slide. "Absolutely nothing. Nothing at all."

Igor nods his head in agreement. "Everything's perfect, your Majesty."

"Then why the dismal looks?"

"You know. Under paid, over worked and unappreciated," said Slide.

"The King stands up and begins to pace. "So, you want more shillings."

"Well of course, said Igor. "But you know; always some little worries with an occasional big one. It is what it is."

"Perhaps you need a lesson in marketing demeanor?"

"What's that," states Igor. "It doesn't sound good at all. Is it a disease?"

"Well, sort of. Let me put something out there for you to consider. Are you ready?"

The King 🪑 McKenzie

Igor and Slide both give a nod, but not with a lot of enthusiasm for their King. The King raises his arms to silence them and to get their attention. "I want you to think about this statement —When you walk into a room, your whole life follows you."

Igor and Slide look at each other. Igor raises his hand and waves to the King's waiter. "I'll have what he's having."

The King raises his hand in the air and signals for two more mugs of watered down wine.

Slide gets up and makes his way to the door. "I'm out of here."

"Slide, may I suggest, as your King, and as your main client, and your biggest client, and at the moment your only client, that you stay and enjoy the refreshment and the lecture I'm about to give."

Slide stops in his tracks, thinks for a minute, spins around and heads for his seat. "Sounds good to me," exclaimed Slide. "Yes, I'll enjoy your Master Class."

"Here we go again," says Igor as he toasts them both with his mug.

The King ignores him. "Now that I have your attention, let's review what I just said, which was, When you walk into a room, your whole life follows you."

Slide, knowing that there is no escape, questions the King. "I have no idea what that means. Can you explain it to me?"

"I'm so happy that you asked. When someone enters the room they bring with them their entire life experience. They bring with them their dreams, desires, disappointments, accomplishments, and they bring their knowledge."

"How does that help me?" asks Slide.

"The King smiles. "The way it helps you is that when you walk into a room you both telegraph to me what you're feeling. Today, you telegraph tiredness, boredom and not wanting to be here for our meeting. You telegraphed you don't care. You telegraphed a wanton disrespect for my position. You telegraphed a non-caring attitude. You know me; you know I want individuals working for me that can contribute to the big picture as well as the tiniest details. I respect your opinion and the ability to get things done. You didn't telegraph that to me."

Igor and Slide are now sitting with good posture listening to their King. "I must say, I'm more then embarrassed," said Igor.

"I have to ask you," said the King, "Do I really want to do business with you based on your entrance, or do I want to business with someone who is enthusiastic about being here, and glad to see me. Someone that has an aura about them, and they literally glow with happiness and success when they make their entrance?"

"Enthusiasm," your Majesty said Igor.

"Yes, you're right. I mean, what if you were going to have open heart surgery and that's the way the Doctor entered the room. How enthusiastic would you be?"

"I would have my doubts. I would be worried. I would not be happy."

"Yes, and there you have it. Be happy. The world will not change because you're worrying about something. But the world will change if you have a positive attitude."

When your executive team walks into a presentation room you're immediately being judged by your behavior. Sometimes deals are lost before anyone speaks a word.

Note: The expression "When you walk into a room . . ." is found in several places on the Internet, but I could find no reference to the origin of the expression as I am using it. It might be me, or I heard it someplace and can't remember.

STORY #67
A Novel Idea

"IT WAS LOVE AT FIRST SIGHT," announced the King.

"What!" said Igor. "Your Majesty, have you fallen in love?"

The King, Igor of Moat Designs and Slide Rule of Building Blocks, Inc. were sitting on a river bank enjoying the early morning sunshine and a spot of tea. Behind them stood several Knights in Shining Armor who were there to protect their King.

"No, no. I was speaking of the river. But even more important, I was reciting the first line of a famous novel by Joseph Heller's *Catch-22*. It was a very clear statement."

"The first line of a famous novel! Now why would you do that?" asked Slide.

"*The moment one learns English, complications set in.*" See, another first line of a famous novel. This one by Felipe Alfau who wrote *Chromos*. Do you have any idea of what my point is about?"

Slide skipped a stone into the river. Several ringlets formed and grew larger and then disappeared. "I have to admit your Majesty; I have no idea of what your point is about. Is it about this river? Is it about the Castle and your first year here?"

"In the late summer of that year we lived in a house in a village that looked across the river and the plain to the mountains."

"Don't tell me?" said Igor. It's another first line."

"Of course; Ernest Hemingway in *A Farewell to Arms*."

"You're speaking in first lines of famous novels. What does this have to do with marketing and business development? That's what you said you wanted to talk to us about."

"In my younger and more vulnerable years my father gave me some advice that I've been turning over in my mind ever since," said the King with a smile.

Igor looked at Slide. He's got us on this one." Igor turned toward the King. "I haven't a clue of what's going on. What novel was that from, your Majesty?"

"*The Great Gatsby* by F. Scott Fitzgerald."

Slide looked at the King. "Regardless of this first line in a novel nonsense, it's a beautiful day. The sun is shining like and giving us warmth. Only the sun can do this, don't you think so, your Majesty?"

"*Far out in the uncharted backwaters of the unfashionable end of the western spiral of the Galaxy lies a small unregarded yellow sun.*"

"I give up. I have no idea what is going on. Perhaps there is another sun?"

"I have no idea your Majesty," Igor stated.

"You should read *The Hitch Hiker's Guide to the Galaxy* by Douglas Adams."

"I see, so that's where the quote came from."

"How about this one. "*It's not fair.*"

Igor threw another rock. "I have no idea of where the quote came from or what this all means."

"It's from *Who Moved The Sun,* by Ron McKenzie." *(shameless self–promotion)*

"Whatever you say, your Majesty.

"*Call me Ishmael,*" responded the King laughing.

Both Igor and Slide are completely confused.

"That was from *Moby-Dick* by Herman Melville."

"This is getting annoying. I hope you have a point someplace that makes some sense. Don't you agree Igor?"

"Completely."

The King turned to both of them and said, "*It was the best of times, it was the worst of times, it was the age of wisdom, it was the age of foolishness, it was the epoch of belief, it was the epoch of incredulity, it was the season of Light, it was the season of Darkness, it was the spring of hope, it was the winter of despair.*"

"Okay. I'm outta here." Slide gets up and Igor follows."

"Wait a minute. I do have a point. But first, that was from *A Tale of Two Cities* by Charles Dickens."

"Doesn't help me one bit said Slide."

"Please sit down. Igor, you said last week that you were developing copy for an ad. Now, tell me, what is the most important thing about an ad?"

"Haven't a clue," said Igor.

"It's the first line. It's the attention getter; the one that's going to get them to read all about your services. I was just demonstrating that point by quoting famous lines from novels. Doesn't that make sense?"

Igor suddenly saw the light of the King's wisdom. "Your Majesty, you have made a good point. You are so right. One must concentrate on the first line of an ad, or even a letter or an electronic email release. It's probably the most basic marketing tactic that is all too often overlooked. You are very tactful. You made something happen just sitting out here by the river."

"How about you, Slide?" said the King.

"All this happened, more or less," said Slide proudly. *Slaughterhouse-Five* by Kurt Vonnegut."

"Good for you Slide," said the King.

As an exercise, copy the first sentence of your website and the important first pages represented by tabs. Also copy the first words of your advertisements as well as your marketing literature and case studies. Are you communicating what you want to say and what image is portrayed?

STORY #68
Shoulda, Coulda, Woulda!

"I HAVE A PROBLEM," said Igor to the King and Slide Rule of Building Blocks, Inc., the head architect for the Castle.

Slide was having Sunday dinner with Igor, from Moat Designs, Ltd., who was the general contractor for the Castle, and also the King of the Castle.

"Another round of brew for everyone," said the King waving his hand in the air. Servants immediately surrounded the party. "What kind of problem are you having, Igor?"

"Well, it's not a big deal. But I'm going to lose some sleep over it."

"Perhaps Slide and I can help you? Why don't you tell us about it? I'm sure we can help."

"I've agreed to write an article for a magazine, and I'm sort of stuck on it. I can't seem to get it going."

"Igor, that's wonderful news. Writing an article for a magazine is one of the best ways to become recognized by your target market? Your business colleagues and potential prospects will respect your opinion, and see you as an expert. You can use it after the article comes out to promote yourself, and you can also say you write for so-and-so magazine."

Slide is now depressed because he wasn't given the opportunity to write an article and get on the good side of the King.

The King pushed himself away from the table. "So, what's the article on, if I may ask? Maybe you can quote me in the article which will give you a lot of credibility."

"I don't know what it's on."

"What do you mean? Didn't the magazine ask you to write something specific?"

"No, they just asked if I would like the opportunity to write for their magazine, and I said yes."

"Well, no matter. I'm sure Slide and I can help. When is your article due?"

Igor tipped his brew and drained it in a long series of gulps.

"Igor. When is it due?" asked the King in a firm voice.

"It's due on Monday."

"Oh, so you've got a week to get it done. You'll be in good shape."

"No, it's due this Monday, not next Monday."

"Tomorrow?"

Slide is now laughing at Igor and very happy.

"Igor, what are you thinking about? You should have started this at least a couple of weeks ago. I don't think I can help you."

"Please, I need your help."

"What magazine is it going to be in?"

"The Farm and Grower Building Gazette."

"Great. I can hardly wait to read it," replied the King sarcastically.

"Your Majesty, I really do need your and Slide's counsel on this problem."

"Well first of all – shoulda, coulda, woulda! You shoulda have started much earlier to get your ideas established, which means you coulda have been done by now, and you woulda have impressed everyone with your professionalism."

"I know."

"So, the first thing you should do is read *Overcoming Procrastination: A 42 Year Report* written by the author of this column. It took over 42 years to write this short report on how writers can overcome procrastination." *(shameless self–promotion of a 99 cent Kindle book).*

"Really."

"Yes, but for you, your first step is to write down all of your ideas, sort of like brainstorming on paper, and then develop those ideas by circling them and then connecting the bubbles together to generate some sort of thesis and sub-points for your article. Next, you need to write a rough draft. Ideally, when you have completed that, you would then read it the next day, and start the editing process."

"Editing?"

"Yes, writing is the art of re-writing. There are not many writers around that can write perfect fresh copy, unless you're Hemingway or some famous author. Do you know what Hemingway said about writing?"

"No. I don't even know anybody named Hemingway."

"He said, '*There is nothing to writing. All you do is sit down at a typewriter and bleed.*'"

"Great, now I'm going to bleed," said Igor.

Another round was served to them and the King quickly removed the chilled mug from in front of Igor. The King waved at a Knight who immediately provided a stick of charcoal to write with and a piece of paper. The King placed them in front of Igor.

"You can take the first step. Don't worry about Igor and I. We're going to be sitting here, along with all my Knights in Shining Armor, Servants and Serfs, watching you create your first article. I know next time you'll plan ahead in writing your article."

"I want to say thank you."

"You want to say thank you?"

"Well, perhaps I should say, shoulda, coulda, woulda."

Planning is what architecture, engineering and construction is all about. But more so, it is what business and life is all about.

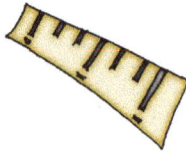

STORY #69
The Comfort Memorandum

SLIDE RULE WALKED INTO THE KING'S CHAMBERS and slumped down on a three-legged stool next to Igor.

"Welcome Slide, my favorite architect of my Kingdom. How are you today?"
"Not so well. In fact, I came here seeking a job."

Igor, the No. 1 moat contractor for the King laughed at Slide. "So, out of work. Maybe the King can give you a job digging ditches?"

"I was thinking I could get a job as a Serf. But that means getting up early and getting to work on time."

"That'll never happen," laughed Igor.

"What's going on Slide?" asked the concerned King. "You're usually quite busy even in slow times."

"Well, I've been ignoring marketing and our marketing genius left, and now, even though I never gave him an audience, he had all the knowledge. I told him things weren't working out. He had the experience to see the big picture and even come up with marketing programs that hardly cost a thing. It's my fault."

"Listen, it's not all that bad. I can help you out, for I, your King, have access to a rather obscure and valuable document known as *The Comfort Memorandum.* It summaries a lot of the important marketing messages I've been lecturing in my Master Class and adds some new tactics to consider."

"Really? Will this document help me?"

"Yes. This information is priceless and will help you to develop marketing programs with minimal expense."

"Let's get started," said Igor. "I can use something like that in my construction business."

"I'm in," said Slide.

"Okay. One important point of *The Comfort Memorandum* concerns your communication materials, including your proposals and qualification statements. I've seen yours Slide, and I've seen yours Igor, and there are too many words and not enough graphics."

"But, I do think what we have works. We haven't changed anything for almost ten years, except we do keep adding to it over time, to make it better," said Igor.

The King raises his hand. "That's the point. See, people don't read. You must convey what you're all about as easily as possible, and that means using graphics, bolded headlines and bullets. If you want to design and build buildings, you first must learn how to design and build your communication material concisely."

"That sounds like a lot of work?" responded Slide.

"Oh, it is. But eventually owners of companies actually learn that marketing is key to their success." The King answered.

Slide Rule was furiously taking notes. "Okay, that's great material, what's another point in *The Comfort Memorandum*?"

"Another important point is about rehearsing your presentations. Let me ask you a question. What do they call firms that don't practice their presentations?"

Slide and Igor look at each other. "We haven't a clue, your Majesty."

"Losers! Those are the people who think they should get the project just because they're such a nice company."

"Really?" said Igor.

"In fact, if you come in second, you have actually won."

"Your Majesty, I'm completely lost." said Slide.

"If you lose, it means you're the number one loser. Remember, you get hired because you can demonstrate that you're the best company for the project. You must show them why you're the best choice. And, to make it more difficult, the presentation must be about them, not about you."

"I'm lost," said Igor. Slide nods his head in agreement.

"This point is not understood by some of the most experienced marketing people out there. It doesn't do any good to list thirty projects that are similar in scope. You must demonstrate, preferably graphically, exactly how your services will benefit them. For example, if the project is simple, like remodeling bathrooms of a facility, then show them examples with photos of what you did and how you did it. Demonstrate to them the problems you've solved, and how your solution saved your client's money. You should have some sketches of their floor plans showing some suggested changes that might reduce their expense, improve their circulation, and improve the overall facility."

"But that's work. I just list the projects that we've done."

"But that's the point. Most people just list thirty bathrooms they've remodeled with a lot of descriptive text. You must show them graphically. People don't read."

"Wow," said Slide. "I've got a lot of work to do."

"This is a simple example but it shows that you must respond to them. Presenters always think it's about them. It's not, it's about the client and how you can help them."

"Your Majesty. We are truly indebted for your help. Speaking for both of us, I can hardly wait to listen to more points of The Comfort Memorandum."

"The ideas in *The Comfort Memorandum* will serve to clarify what's important, and what isn't important in marketing your services. It's not hard at all. In fact, it's comfortable"

The Comfort Memorandum is all around you. Read, study and become a student of the construction delivery process. Learn how others make presentations, study web sites that have recorded presentations as part of the public bidding process, attend other presentations and take notes and learn. As you do, record what works for you, and over time, you will have your own Comfort Memorandum.

Author Note: The Comfort Memorandum is a new book planned to be published in 2016. The book is based on bringing Comfort to Companies by organizing their marketing and planning.

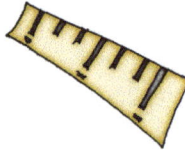

The King 🪑 McKenzie

ONE LAST THOUGHT

IN ORDER TO PROVIDE STRUCTURE I have chosen to divide the contents between Strategy, Business Planning and Marketing. There is tremendous overlap between the three areas; however, it does provide an infrastructure to better grasp the material. Certainly, everyone understands what strategy is all about, but do they really know what the difference between Strategy and the Business Plan? Meanwhile, most view Marketing as an expense. The diagram at the beginning of each section pulls these together and provides a visual representation of the relationships.

I believe that all companies can gain a significant strategic advantage with planning that will impact the bottom line. Clearly, strategy drives marketing. With that said, other questions need to be asked, such as, why should a company hire your company as opposed to your competition? An even better question is, why does a company sign with your competition even thought their price is higher? (The answer is hidden in your competitor's value offering.) I also believe that no matter what the challenges you have before you in your business, business and marketing planning is a key resource in implementing future identified changes or projects to get to where you want to go.

The wrong reason to develop or revisit a business/marketing plan is because a consultant says it's the thing to do. The main reason why business planning works is hidden in the planning process. It's the process that is so important; as it's the process that's the secret embedded within business planning. It's the process that forces a company to examine all of the issues facing them, so they can develop strategy and tactics to accomplish their goals. All those that participate in the origination of the strategy take ownership of the plan that they will be responsible for implementing.

The one question I'm often asked, is: Where does a company start? My answer is: Where do you hurt? What part of your business needs attention? My methodology allows you to start anywhere so that critical areas are immediately addressed. If it is a marketing challenge to develop new prospects, then that's where you should start.

The origin of many business challenges is often deeply rooted in a company's culture. Strategy, marketing, operations, finance, project management, human resources, ownership transition, and other areas of a company often are only reflections of that company's culture. There is always resistance to change. The dynamics of a true planning process is that people began to understand what the company culture is all about, and take ownership of their own areas of responsibility as well as helping others with their areas of responsibility. When this happens an immediate transformation takes place, and as a result, the company is suddenly much more productive. The result is bottom line improvement.

This company renewal can only happen within a planning process guided by someone who knows and understands the construction environment, understands the dynamics of the planning process, and can actually produce the plan that will lead to implementation. This transformation leads to enhanced communications by everyone.

Every industry has their unique values, and the construction industry usually compete using the values such as design, planning, best people, and expertise in a market niche, etc., but this is a losing situation, as everyone does this. Companies need to create "competitive advantages," so the prospect seeks you out well before your competition even knows about the project. This advantage must be marketed — sometimes in very subliminal ways. To me, the entire focus of my consulting comes down to those two words — competitive advantage. A company must be perceived as offering something of value that the competition is not offering. People buy for three reasons, one is they can make money, two, they can save money, or three, they buy from you because they want to work with you. That's because you have a real competitive advantage; they only want to work with your company.

For all my readers, whether it be my columns or my books, I would like to say thank you for your letters, emails and telephone calls.

I WOULD LIKE TO MAKE THE FOLLOWING OFFER TO MY READERS: if you send me an email I'll forward you a **BUSINESS PLAN OUTLINE** that has endured the test of time, and will be a perfect tool to review your own plan, or to start a new one. You might find this a valuable tool for your own business adventures.

I WOULD ALSO LIKE TO MAKE A SECOND OFFER. If you are looking for a way to compete that is so different that it absolutely shocks your competitors, call me and I'll explain the concept to you. You can either do it yourself, or I can help you, but it will give you leverage that will help you close more business deals. As part of my relationship with all my clients, I include a non-disclosure clause as well as a non-compete clause, meaning, first come, first served, and the only one served. I would not do this for any of your competitors, and I review and screen all inquirers very seriously to avoid any conflict of interest.

And, who knows, maybe you'll become the King!

Ronald A. McKenzie, NCARB
630 740-4434
ramckenzie.compass@gmail.com
www. compassconsultantscorp.com
www.bd4aec.org

A REMINDER – EVERYONE WANTS MORE!
STORY #70 – We Want More!

"YOU'VE REALLY RAMPED UP YOUR MARKETING," said the King to So, Igor.

"What's going on?"

The King, Igor, the contractor for the Castle and Owner of Moat Designs, and Slide Rule, the head architect and owner of Building Blocks, were all sitting on top the highest point in the Castle looking at the incredible view of the river and farm fields all owned by the King. They were all excitedly watching for the arrival of another load of granite blocks from the quarry for the Castle's newest addition.

"We want more!" said Igor out of the blue.

The King turned toward Igor and gave him a strange look. "You want more what?"

"More. We want more. More is better."

The King was a bit lost. "What do you mean?"

"I'm talking about my business. I want more work."

"If you want more, then are you doing those things we've been talking about in this book?"

"Yes. I've been implementing and it's working. I wish all businesses understood the value of what I do to grow my company and increase profits."

"Can you expound on your wisdom for your friend Slide, and tell him your philosophy for growth?"

"Well, if you have less, then that is bad. We want more."

"But wanting more doesn't get you there," said the King.

"True. I just know I want more, and that works for me."

Slide listened to his friend Igor. "I think that's one of the smartest things you've ever said, Igor. But I need to ask, does it work in a slow or recovering economy?"

Igor started to get excited. "It works even better when companies around you are having problems. They generally don't market when they don't have work. So, that puts me ahead of the game and my marketing shillings go further."

The King got up and started to pace. "You're so right Igor. How about if I outline what you've been doing so Slide really understands the significance of your accomplishments?"

"I would appreciate that very much," replied Igor.

So, the King in all his glory took center stage in front of his two students. Another Master Class was in session. "First, you must have a plan. Remember, it was Thomas A. Edison who said, *'Vision without execution is hallucination.'*"

Slide's hand immediately shot up. "Your Majesty, who's he?"

"Don't worry. A bright light will turn on someday and you'll know. Now, there are basically three things you've been doing Igor, even if you don't know it, that has made you successful. First, having a well thought out planning process is critical. Let me borrow a phrase from one of the foremost construction business planning experts in the United States who writes this column, Ron McKenzie, *(yes, shameless self–promotion)*, who said the following at a speech recently In San Antonio, Texas."

"And I quote…as a review:"

> *"All companies can gain a significant strategic advantage with planning that will impact their bottom line.*

*A <u>strategic plan</u> provides direction for a company and
its employees for three-to-five years based upon developing
a company strategy of where your company wants to be in
terms of positioning in your marketplace.*

*The <u>business plan</u> says, based upon the strategic plan, this
is what we're all going to do this year to work toward
accomplishing the strategic plan. This means the
business plan is an annual document addressed
every year.*

*A <u>marketing plan</u> is what you're going to do this year to
support the business plan, and in turn, support the
long-range objectives of the strategic plan."*

The King finished speaking and looked up at his faithful audience of two.

"Well, what do you think?"

Igor responded. "Yes, you're right, that's exactly what I do. I have a strategic,
business and marketing plan, and we use them as our primary management
tool. That's how we came up with our firm's internal mission statement."

"What is that?" asked Slide.

"We want more!"

**If you want more, plan for more. It can't get any simpler —
that's what business planning is all about.**

Note: The inspiration for this column came from AT&T's "It's Not Complicated"
ad campaign in their entertaining TV commercial "We Want More" developed
by BBDO, NYC and BBDO Atlanta. All referenced product names and marks
are trademarks of their respective owners and are hereby acknowledged.

AUTHOR BIO

RONALD A. MCKENZIE, NCARB is a licensed architect in California and is president of **COMPASS Consultants Corporation,** a national strategic planning company for the construction industry.

Ron has practiced architecture in his firm in the San Francisco Bay area in California, and worked in Steamboat Springs, Colorado for an architect, as well as for a thirty person architectural firm as a business developer, and for a major Chicago based design-build company.

Ron has also worked for multi-million dollar corporations traveling and making high level corporate presentations for NCR and AM International in one of their respective product sales divisions.

He has traveled to most major cities in the United States speaking at seminars and conventions on business planning and marketing. He's also traveled to Hong Kong, Tokyo and Paris to train sales people and to make presentations.

At one company he reported to the Director of Sales for the Western Region, Bert Torres, who was an Army Green Beret officer in charge of several A Teams. Bert and Ron traveled together meeting their sales teams and making presentations with them. At night, after the sales associates had left, Bert and Ron talked about military strategy and intelligence gathering (competitive intelligence). Ironically, it was Bert Torres who first introduced to him the concepts of business planning. Bert also introduced him to Sun Tzu and The Art of War and they discussed military tactics as it applies to business.

Ron was first published by McGraw-Hill in 1991 with his book **Successful Business Plans for Architects** with Bruce H. Schoumacher of the Chicago based law firm of Querrey & Harrow, Ltd. He then developed his story telling techniques by writing screenplays with his identical twin brother when Don was working for **Entertainment Tonight.** They then authored together the **Fargo Blue Mystery Series** – the first one was **Poolside Sting** published by Infinity, and then the second one was **Coyote Trap,** which was self-published under D.E.M. Publishing. Ron also wrote a biography called **Who Moved The Sun: A Twin Remembers.** In addition, Ron wrote **Overcoming Procrastination: A 42 Year Project** on techniques to overcoming procrastination.

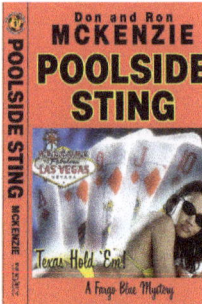
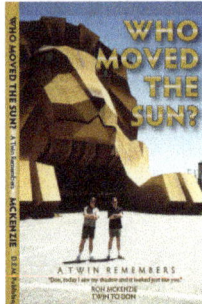
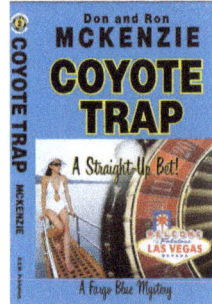

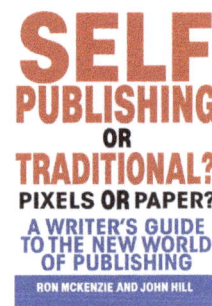

Ron McKenzie and Emmy award winning screenplay author John Hill recently published **Self Publishing VS. Traditional Publishing? Pixels or Paper?** The book helps sort out the options writers have in the new digital publishing world. There now exists a new, complicated set of publishing choices, from an e-Book or Kindle, to self-published trade size books, as well as using traditional publishers. By examining what you expect to get from your publishing experience, and by examining the different Paper or Pixel options available to you, you can determine how to bring your book to market.

The King 👑 McKenzie

Ron lives with his wife Pamela in Las Vegas, not very far away from the most famous Castle in the Las Vegas desert, where much of the inspiration for the King and the moat contractor started. He continues to consult with companies across the United States, and speak at tradeshows and seminars. You can reach him at any time if you have questions about business planning and marketing.

Ronald A. McKenzie
COMPASS Consultants Corporation
630-740-4434
ramckenzie.compass@gmail.com
www.compassconsultantscorp.com
www.bd4aec.org

THE KING'S MASTER CLASS
The King and the Moat Contractor
Strategy, Business Planning and Marketing
"For All Businesses and Industries"

MANY TIMES, TEXTBOOKS AVOID THE THINKING PART. This book is about getting you to think about strategic planning, business planning and marketing.

The King's lessons apply to all businesses and industries. Whether you're in real estate, a retail store front, a restaurant, an association, an attorney, a doctor, or an Internet company, the lessons of the King will give you a competitive advantage. You will start thinking differently and you'll start to plan, instead of react.

Thinking is the KEY; thinking and applying the concepts to your business, or to your life, is the secret. You will look forward to implementing, instead of avoiding implementing.

You can change, you can improve; you can make a difference.

These stories are short and the business concepts are summarized at the end. Take a few minutes each day and read one, and it will change your business thinking. The King and the Moat Contractor is an excellent source of ideas for those that are learning the sales, business development and marketing roles of a business. It gets them to THINK about the big picture in a different way from normal textbooks.

www.ingramcontent.com/pod-product-compliance
Lightning Source LLC
Chambersburg PA
CBHW042314210326
41599CB00038B/7123